THE MAN
WHO LEAPT
THROUGH
FILM
THE ART OF
MAMORU HOSODA

THE MAN WHO LEAPT THROUGH FILM

THE ART OF MAMORU HOSODA

BY CHARLES SOLOMON

FOREWORD BY DON HAHN

ABRAMS
NEW YORK

CONTENTS

FOREWORD

Animation is a complicated web of technology, artistry, and storytelling that many have tried and few have mastered. It's an elaborate illusion made from pencils, paint, and pixels that, at its best, allows us to escape reality. Mamoru Hosoda uses the art form in a different way. He dives into reality with characters who are vulnerable, who may live in unimaginable worlds, but who always feel grounded in the very human themes that often resonate in his work: consequence, responsibility, sacrifice, hope.

Hosoda has carved out a personal style that bridges anime and sci-fi, yet he and his collaborators tell stories that are remarkably human, given his penchant for setting them in mind-bending worlds that threaten humanity. His work opens our eyes to the complex choices we face in a life that is overwhelmed by often inhumane forces. Like all good science fiction, his films are relevant and even predictive of our future on a planet that is changing incredibly fast.

Any filmmaker can fall victim to his or her comfortable and predictable patterns, like a magician who does the same trick so often that the audience starts to see how it's done. Hosoda's work builds on his past, but reliably manages to make a fresh statement that always surprises me. He directs with a fearless mix of subtle introspection, grandiose spectacle, and a master storyteller's disregard for time and space. As such he has built a reputation for expanding the animated art form, most recently by fostering unconventional collaborations with people like Irish filmmakers Tomm Moore and Ross Stewart, visionary UK architect Eric Wong, and my friend, the brilliant designer Jin Kim.

The audience may never fully appreciate the incredible artistry, technology, and just plain hard work that goes into Hosoda's films, and maybe that's how it should be. But after nine films, it's time to take a closer look. Here, Charles Solomon takes us inside the filmmaker's sanctum to reveal the intense art and craft that make us believe the unbelievable and discover new levels of our human condition through the work of this incredible artist.

Don Hahn
April 27, 2021

PREVIOUS SPREAD **Ame frolics in the snow in these animation drawings from** *Wolf Children.*

OPPOSITE **Swathed in a cloud of pink blossoms, Belle reflects during a song.**

DON HAHN produced the classic *Beauty and the Beast*, the first animated film to receive a Best Picture nomination from the Academy of Motion Pictures Arts and Sciences. His next film, *The Lion King*, broke box-office records all over the world to become the top-grossing traditionally animated film of all time and a long-running blockbuster Broadway musical. Hahn also served as associate producer on the landmark motion picture *Who Framed Roger Rabbit*. His other films include *The Hunchback of Notre Dame*, *Atlantis: The Lost Empire*, the 2006 short *The Little Matchgirl* (which earned Hahn his second Oscar nomination), *Maleficent*, and Tim Burton's *Frankenweenie*. He directed the documentaries *Waking Sleeping Beauty*, *Hand Held*, *The Gamble House*, and *Howard*. Hahn is the author of *The Alchemy of Animation*, *Brain Storm: Unleashing Your Creative Self*, *Before Ever After: The Lost Lectures of Walt Disney's Animation Studio*, and *Yesterday's Tomorrow: Disney's Magical Mid-Century*. He lives in Los Angeles.

I. EARLY DAYS 細田守の初期

The first thing I bought with my own money was the November 1979 issue of *Animage*, with Lupin III on the cover. I went to see *The Castle of Cagliostro* in the theater; after watching it, I couldn't think of anything else. Thanks to *Animage*, I knew about the people who made the film, like Miyazaki. For a "What Do I Want to Become When I Grow Up" essay in sixth grade, I said, "animation director."

—MAMORU HOSODA

Mamoru Hosoda was born on September 19, 1967, in

Kamiichi, a small town in the Toyama Prefecture in mountainous western Japan. The son of a railway engineer, he remembers watching cartoons in kindergarten, particularly the mecha series *Mazinger Z*. He recalls, "I preferred animated robots to superheroes. I started drawing with my kindergartener's hands; I even tried tracing my toys, which turned out badly."

An only child, Hosoda was introduced by an older friend to Leiji Matsumoto's seminal science-fiction epic, *Space Battleship Yamato* (released as *Star Blazers* in the United States), which left a lasting impression: "It just boomed all over Japan. I was part of the boom and contributed to it. The scope and magnitude of the film were so fascinating."

Like other young artists, Hosoda's interest was stimulated in middle school by *Animage*, the pioneering animation magazine edited by Toshio Suzuki. On television, Hosoda watched the boxing saga *Tomorrow's Joe 2* (1980), directed by Osamu Dezaki; Rintaro's feature *Galaxy Express 999* (1979); and Mamoru Oshii's *Urusei Yatsura 2: Beautiful Dreamer* (1984), which blended elements of the Urashima Tarō folktale with Rumiko Takahashi's sci-fi comedy series.

In his third year of middle school, Hosoda made his first animated film after seeing work by aspiring artists on the educational program *You*. Until then, he had thought of animation as "something I just sat and watched." Using a makeshift light box with pieces of chopsticks for pegs, he did nine hundred drawings, which he filmed on a rented Fuji 8mm camera.

"A dragon appears in a lake: Out of nowhere, multiple fighter jets fly in, launching missiles," Hosoda recalls. "The dragon fights back, breathing flames that destroy the fighters. One fighter delivers a final blow: The dragon is injured and some of its scales are torn off, revealing it's really a mecha. It didn't have much of a story, but lots of explosions. My only motivation was to make a combat scene."

Although he screened the film at his school cultural festival, Hosoda was less interested in his classmates' reactions than the satisfaction of making and seeing the film. But during his first year of high school, the period adventure film *Kenya Boy* (*Shonen Keniya*) included a call for independent animators to send their work to the Toei studio. Hosoda submitted his film.

"One day, I came home and my mother said I'd gotten 'a weird call from Tokyo,'" he says. "It was from Toei producer Takeshi Tamiya. It was my first call from Tokyo, and from a producer! I was dancing with joy. The next day, I nervously phoned Toei. Of the approximately thirty videos sent in, Tamiya picked mine as number one.

"Tamiya said, 'You've got a lot of potential. Do you want to come try something out? You've got to come to Tokyo for it,'" Hosoda continues. "The day coincided with one of my midterms, so I had to decline, and someone else got it. But after I graduated from university, Tamiya helped me find my way into Toei."

During his second year of high school, Hosoda made another film: "I wanted to create a mecha explosion with broken pieces bouncing all over the surface of earth—my take on *Macross* [released in the US as part of *Robotech*]," he says. "It took roughly three thousand drawings. I studied the smoke from the God Warrior Hideaki Anno animated in *Nausicaä*

9

of the Valley of the Wind: I was studying the *Art of Nausicaä* book while I was doing it. I didn't even screen it at the school festival; I saw it on my own, and that was it. But I have the film somewhere."

During junior high school, Hosoda became more interested in painting, especially landscapes in the Western tradition. He wanted his paintings to depict "lived-in spaces, where people breathed life into the places," a quality he would later seek in the backgrounds for his films. A part-time teacher at his high school took an interest in Hosoda and gave him lessons in sketching at her home after school.

He studied painting at Kanazawa College of Art, where he and future advertising art director Katsuhiko Suzuki formed a film group. "We called it 'Yotsuki-rocket-dan,' a name like something out of *Pokémon*," Hosoda says. "This is where I started making movies." The two friends wrote scripts, filmed their classmates, and snuck into a school building to edit their films at night—dousing the lights when the watchman went by.

After graduation, Hosoda couldn't find openings in the film industry to apply for. After a brief, unsuccessful stab at advertising, he took the entrance exam at Studio Ghibli. "I was handed a sheet of paper with a boy's face on it; I had to draw the body of the boy lifting a large rock. It was to test the kind of poses I drew," Hosoda says. "Later, I received a letter from Hayao Miyazaki that said, 'Your talents would be wasted if we were to accept you.' I was so frustrated, I phoned Ghibli begging to be hired as an entry-level clerk. One of the production staff told me that of all the people who had taken the test, Miyazaki had only written to two, so please accept it and be quiet. As I had no other choice, I contacted Tamiya."

With Tamiya's support, Hosoda began at Toei as an animator. He wanted to be a director, and there were few opportunities. "I was excited to join Toei, but the studio was going through financial struggles tied to a downturn in the world economy," he explains. "They were working with overseas companies on a lot of co-productions like *Transformers* and *Jem* because the low exchange rate had been very favorable. But the yen

Hosoda as a little boy in Toyama

RIGHT **Hosoda's junior high essay: "I want to be an animation director."**

FAR RIGHT **One of Hosoda's high school landscapes: He insisted his paintings show "lived-in spaces."**

Hosoda (in the black shirt) and some of his animator friends share a meal.

became so powerful relative to the other currencies that working on these co-productions put them in the red. Plus, we were in a recession: The networks had cut their usual order of five or six TV series to maybe three, which left an excess of directors, narrowing my opportunities.

"It was a very challenging time at Toei," he adds. "A lot of people asked, 'Why'd you join? You're boarding a sinking ship. The atmosphere felt like something you'd see in a Western, where a tumbleweed rolls across the empty street and coyotes howl in the distance.'"

Toei's fortunes were buoyed by the runaway success of the *Sailor Moon* TV series in 1992. Hosoda did animation for various features and broadcast programs, including 1993's *From a Distant Ocean Came Coo*, the *Dragon Ball Z* show, and the eighth *Dragon Ball Z* feature, *Broly – The Legendary Super Saiyan* (1993).

During that time, Hosoda says, "I learned a lot from the animator in the room next to mine, Takaaki Yamashita. His work was so amazing! My skills just couldn't compare, and I felt there was no way I'd be able to stay there. I got Yamashita to check my work; after some time, he asked if I'd like to go onto the OVA (original video animation) *Crying Freeman 5* (1992) as key animator. I'd started at Toei just a year earlier."

"I suppose I was Hosoda's *senpai* [senior] in the sense that I had joined Toei earlier," Yamashita, who would later serve as animation director on *Wolf Children* and *The Boy and the Beast*, replies modestly. "He started off as an animator, but would always want to add that little bit of direction; that was the direction he was going in."

Hosoda became friends with other young artists who got together regularly to talk about animation. He feels

he learned a great deal, "not from hitting the books, but by having tea and chatting and having fun." The friends also spent a lot of time playing Sega's *Virtua Fighter*, the first 3-D fighting game. "We weren't playing *Virtua Fighter* between work hours: It seemed like we were working between *Virtua Fighter* sessions," Hosoda says. "Next to Toei was an arcade where we would drop ¥5000 [about $50.00] daily on games. We were kind of nuts."

Shingo Kaneko, one of his *Virtua Fighter* friends, gave Hosoda a chance to try storyboarding: "One day, Shingo said, 'These tight deadlines are difficult to work around, and I can't handle things alone; won't you give me a hand?' She gave me the opportunity to do storyboards for *Twelve Warrior Explosive Eto Rangers*. I was under contract to Toei as an animator, but we didn't believe storyboarding for another company was a breach of contract."

Hosoda was disappointed when he saw the finished program he had storyboarded. But the producers asked him to board two more episodes. He also worked on Kazuhiro Furuhashi's OVA *Rurouni Kenshin: Trust & Betrayal* (1999) using an alternate spelling of his name as a pseudonym. The four-part adventure explored the backstory of reformed assassin Kenshin Himura. Hosoda notes the "other" Hosoda called it one of his great achievements.

After the success of *Sailor Moon*, series director Kunihiko Ikuhara developed a new program, *Revolutionary Girl Utena*. Several episodes were storyboarded by Katsuyo Hashimoto—another pseudonym, this one based on Hosoda's grandmother's name. But when he saw fellow artist Hiroshi Nishikiori's storyboards, he was so impressed with the drawings, he felt a rivalry. Work became so stressful, Hosoda's hair fell out.

"In my storyboards, the Juri Arisugawa character, a conflicted Student Council Duelist, became my alter ego," he remembers. "I was depressed at the prospect of having to wear a hat for the rest of my life, but I had this battle that I needed to win."

Hosoda complained to Ikuhara that the script for the twenty-ninth episode didn't end Juri's story properly. The director gave him permission to rewrite it, as long as the boards were completed on deadline. The screenwriting credit for the episode is Chiaki Shirai, another Hosoda pseudonym. As soon as he concluded Juri's story arc, his hair started to grow back.

Hosoda moved on to *GeGeGe no Kitarō*, the fourth television adaptation of Shigeru Mizuki's popular manga originally known as *Hakaba Kitaro*, "Kitarō of the Graveyard." He was promoted to director's assistant on the thirty-eighth episode. The series introduced Hosoda to the possibilities digital technology offered animation.

Since the silent era, animators had drawn their characters on paper; the drawings were traced onto clear acetate cels and photographed. Disney had begun scanning the artists' drawings into computers and coloring them digitally on *The Rescuers Down Under* in 1990. The Japanese animation industry continued using cels for several years.

"Toei's philosophy towards digitization was different from other companies: They embraced it to reduce costs and labor, not to advance a new technology," Hosoda comments. "The work wasn't handled in-house, but subcontracted. The director and director's assistant would look over the rushes; when they agreed retakes were needed, the assistant would call up the subcontractors."

Hosoda was promoted to director on "Kitarō's Fish and the Moat," the ninety-fourth episode of *GeGeGe no Kitarō*. "Kitarō's Fish Market," the first of three episodes he would direct, aired on November 9, 1997—two months after his thirtieth birthday. As a director's assistant, Hosoda had carefully watched the different approaches directors used with voice actors. As a director, he supervised the dubbing, sound effects, and music for each episode, which taught him the importance of sound in filmmaking.

"I 'aggressively' rely on sound effects in my films, especially for things that occur off-camera," he says. "By doing so, I can expand the world being developed. I make sure to think about sound effects during the storyboarding process, and we spend a lot of time discussing sound during meetings. I think I spend double the normal time on dubbing and sound."

As *GeGeGe no Kitarō* neared its conclusion, Hosoda was shifted to *Akko-chan's Secret 3*, the third animated adaptation of Fujio Akatsuka's manga about a little girl whose magic mirror enables her to transform into anything she chooses. Hosoda spent two months struggling with his first episode.

But on a later episode, he grasped that because the title character "was not that intelligent; she'd stick her nose

I have to thank *Sailor Moon*'s breakaway success for where I am right now. Initially, I made fun of *Sailor Moon*, saying this is why Toei is going to fail. I want to retract all those statements; I'm very, very thankful for what it's done for me. It was a very humbling experience to see that kind of success. It offered a really good opportunity for me to study what the directors of *Sailor Moon* were doing to make it such a success.

—MAMORU HOSODA

into all sorts of situations and mess up. I realized there's a way to make an unintelligent character fun to watch, which I used in *The Girl Who Leapt Through Time*." Hosoda also used his time on *Akko-chan* to explore digital and other animation techniques, sometimes drawing on the talents of his friends from the *Virtua Fighter* group.

When Hosoda returned to Tokyo after attending his father's funeral in Toyama, *Akko-chan*'s producer Hiromi Seki approached him about directing a movie. "I didn't even ask anything about it before saying I'd do it," he says. "It turned out to be *Digimon Adventure*, the first short feature; I started at the end of September 1998. I had no clue what *Digimon* was about. From the name, I guessed it must be something like *Pokémon*. The assistant producer had to teach me what 'Digital Monsters' were."

"We were slated to open amid a glut of monster movies: *Gamera 3: Revenge of Iris* and *Ultraman Tiga: The Final Odyssey* were all being released during spring break," Hosoda says. "The 'suits' at the distributor asked me to make *Digimon* into a monster movie; they didn't realize that *Digimon* was competing with *Pokémon,* which was on TV, not those Godzilla-style theatrical movies."

The filmmakers were charged with adapting the "Digital Monsters" from the Bandai portable LCD toy. Hosoda asked to modify the designs of Greymon and Agumon, which Bandai okayed. The script wasn't approved until the beginning of November; the storyboards had to be completed by New Year's. Hosoda notes, "We knew we were in for a real time crunch."

The main human characters were kids who lived in modern Tokyo apartments, with their thirtysomething parents. Hosoda confesses, "I was thirty-one and had no clue how households with kids were furnished. I started looking at apartments for rent or sale. I knew a single male looking for a family-style apartment would appear suspicious, so I had a female staff member come with me."

The team managed to complete *Digimon* on schedule but overshot the allotted number of drawings by about

50 percent. The overages ruffled feathers in the production department, but Hosoda felt his crew's work put them at the forefront of the Japanese animation industry.

Digimon Adventure premiered on March 6, 1999. The film served as a prologue to the broadcast series, introducing Takeru "Tai" Kamiya and his sister Kari (Taichi and Hikari Yagami in the original Japanese) and the other kids who form the "DigiDestined." They find a Digi-egg that hatches Tyrannosaurus-like Greymon, who battles the avian Parrotmon at the film's climax.

Although the film used CGI (computer-generated imagery) in a few scenes, Hosoda says, "It wasn't until the following year that we finally had a proper CG department in the company—and a proper budget to work with. We really used CG in *Digimon*."

Hosoda continued experimenting with computer graphics and worked on *Digimon* shorts before turning to the second featurette, *Digimon: Our War Game!* In *Our War Game!* Tai and his friend Izzy (Koshiro Izumi in Japanese) discover a Digimon egg in cyberspace; when it hatches, Diaboromon turns out to be a living malware. It devours data, gobbling lines of code like a renegade Pac-Man. Its depredations cause problems in the real world, affecting phones, home computers, and cash registers in stores. Universal Product Codes on merchandise shift in simple but effective visuals.

As Diaboromon grows in power, it launches a US Peacekeeper missile at Japan (the film was partially inspired by John Badham's 1983 *WarGames*). Tai and Matt battle Diaboromon in cyberspace; their Digimon fuse to form a super-fighter unnamed in the film but later dubbed "Omegamon" by Bandai. Izzy asks people all over the world to send emails to Diaboromon, which

Izzy, Tai, and Greymon prepare to tackle the unseen Diaboromon in *Digimon: Our War Game!* The stylized background anticipates the look of both the Louis Vuitton promotional film and OZ in *Summer Wars*.

slows him down; Omegamon delivers the coup de grâce with a sword, and the disarmed missile splashes harmlessly into Tokyo Bay.

Only forty minutes long, *Digimon: Our War Game!* was released on March 4, 2000, on a double bill with *One Piece: The Movie* and earned an impressive ¥2.16 billion (more than $20 million). Hosoda notes that Isao Takahata's *My Neighbors the Yamadas* (1999) was the first digital Japanese animated feature; *Our War Game!* was the second. It remains the most discussed of Hosoda's early films, as the story and the visual styles anticipate *Summer Wars*: Both films involve battles in the Web that have real-world consequences, and Hosoda uses mundane elements to demonstrate the connections between the everyday and cyber worlds. The Digimon fight in a white cyberspace filled with rotating, bright pastel rings that suggest Ferris wheels, anticipating the Superflat look of the cyber realm of OZ in *Summer Wars*. *Our War Game!* is an entertaining installment in a popular franchise, but it bears the same relation to the far more sophisticated *Summer Wars* that a preliminary sketch does to a painting.

Our War Game! attracted a lot of interest and brought the filmmaker an unexpected offer. "Toshio Suzuki from Ghibli called me," Hosoda says. "They were looking for an up-and-coming director for *Howl's Moving Castle*. I was thirty-three years old, and it was my chance to direct my first feature-length film. I knew working at Ghibli was going to be different from Toei. There was a little anxiety there.

TOP RIGHT **Hosoda at work at Toei**

ABOVE RIGHT **His desk at Toei: quite tidy by animators' standards**

RIGHT **The cast of the popular girls' series *Magical Doremi Dokkān*: Hosoda's work as an episode director impressed Masao Maruyama, the co-founder of the Madhouse studio.**

The bright pastel colors against the white background gave the Louis Vuitton film an immediate appeal.

But being a huge fan of their movies, I responded with a resounding 'yes.'"

Pre-production work on *Howl* did not go well. The Ghibli artists were used to working for two of the most celebrated directors in world animation, Hayao Miyazaki and Isao Takahata; Hosoda was regarded as a newcomer and an outsider. His attempts to make the film his way met with resistance.

"I started at Ghibli on August 1, 2000; I was fired April 21, 2002, and returned to Toei," he says. "Senior managing director of production Osamu Yoshioka took me aside and said, 'You must have gone through many difficult things; why don't you switch to TV for a change of pace and take it easier for a bit.'"

Hosoda went to work on a series already in production, *Magical Doremi Dokkān*. At the same time, his friend Shingo Kaneko began directing *Spiral: The Bonds of Reasoning*, so one Katsuyo Hashimoto helped out with the opening. In November 2002, Takashi Murakami approached Toei about collaborating on an advertising film for the luxury brand Louis Vuitton. As Murakami was famous for blurring

the boundaries of high and low art, Hosoda realized the project would inevitably generate controversy, but he felt it could promote contemporary art in Japan.

"They had difficulties hammering out a concept until they showed the Vuitton people artwork from *War Game*: That look matched what they wanted to showcase in their spring/summer collection," Hosoda explains. "Murakami, [former Vuitton creative director] Marc Jacobs, and I agreed we wanted to create something visually stimulating. Even if the audience didn't necessarily have an interest in anime, the visuals would be so bizarre, they would have no choice but to watch. I found the collaboration very stimulating."

A few months later, Murakami approached Hosoda again, this time for a commercial for the Roppongi Hills project: a huge city-within-a-city development project in Tokyo that would include offices, shops, entertainment facilities, parks, and residences, centered on the fifty-four-story Mori Tower. Hosoda was going through a bad time and initially declined.

"I later accepted; the concept was wide open, except they wanted to use an alien with the building," he says. "My concept was to have a giant vine wrap around things, then suddenly blossom into a giant bouquet. I thought that even though cities may be razed to the ground, they will be born again through human effort, blessed with even greater beauty. When I was invited to the official launch of the ad campaign, I realized the new building would become a Tokyo landmark. I was happy to be part of it, and the commercial was well received."

At the same time, Hosoda directed three episodes of *Tomorrow's Nadja*, as well as a commercial for the video game *Slime Morimori Dragon Quest*. Then the Toei management asked him to salvage a project that was floundering under a novice director.

"They didn't expect the project to turn out good, but they wanted to at least complete it some way," Hosoda sighs. "It was an all-hands-on-deck emergency, so I did as much as I could. But the key takeaway was that sometimes the world presents you with problems like this. After that unfortunate project was completed, I thought it would be the perfect opportunity to announce I was quitting.

"When I had returned to Toei, I talked with Toei's senior managing director, Mr. Yoshioka, who said, 'Toei is like a school for young artists: I can't let you quit without making at least one feature film. Why don't you quit after directing a One Piece feature,'" Hosoda continues. "It wasn't because Toei was short-staffed and had no one who could direct it. I think the people at Toei wanted to send me off with one feature-length film under my belt."

One Piece: Baron Omatsuri and the Secret Island (2005), the sixth theatrical feature in the hugely popular franchise, sends Luffy and the Straw Hat Pirates to mysterious Omatsuri Island. The Baron convinces them to participate in the "Trial of Hell" contest, which leads to complications and fights and a surprise conclusion. *Baron Omatsuri* opened to good business, although fans note it plays more like a Hosoda film than a typical *One Piece* movie.

Hiroyuki Aoyama, who would later be a character designer and animation director on *Belle*, recalls, "I was at a company called Telecom, and I met Hosoda on the *One Piece* movie. As I worked on just two scenes, I only saw him briefly in meetings. But the success of *Digimon: Our War Game!* had already made him famous; people were saying how wonderful his skills were, that he had a bright future. I was a little nervous around him."

Around that time, Masao Maruyama, the co-founder of Madhouse, saw an episode Hosoda had directed of *Magical Doremi Dokkān*. "He sent me an email saying, 'You were meant to make movies,'" Hosoda recalls. "When we met, I broached the idea of making *The Girl Who Leapt Through Time* into a film. Maruyama said, 'That's a good idea, I'm on board to make that film.' When he said that, I made the decision to leave Toei.

"I was transitioning to Madhouse; Maruyama kept insisting we should do something based on a manga, or take one of Wagner's operas and adapt it into an animated movie, which was an interesting idea but not exactly what I wanted to do," Hosoda says. "While Maruyama and I continued discussing the plans to make *The Girl Who Leapt Through Time* together, he said, 'Before we work together on this big project, there's another project that would be the perfect thing to prepare you for it.'"

The project was Shinichirō Watanabe's *Samurai Champloo*, the follow-up to his smash hit *Cowboy Bebop*. *Champloo* mixed Edo-era samurai, Hiroshima homeboys, and Tokugawa hip-hop in an outrageous cross-cultural mash-up. Hosoda recalls, "We had a meeting with Watanabe, and he described it as taking place in the Edo period but in an exaggerated, over-the-top style. He asked me to make the opening sequence, which is what I was in charge of, as wild and crazy as I could."

He did. Hosoda storyboarded and directed the opening of the first episode, using a surprising series of flashbacks and flashforwards to introduce the motley trio of main characters: steely ronin Jin; Fuu, a maladroit waitress; and breakdancing brawler Mugen. *Samurai Champloo* also introduced Hosoda to his future producer, Yuichiro Saito, whom he recalls as "a very young and energetic producer of twenty-seven. Wide-eyed and fresh, just coming into the industry."

Saito had been working at Madhouse for four years. He'd gotten into animation because he'd been moved by the Ghibli films and *Barefoot Gen*—human dramas that conveyed deeper messages. He was tired of the action series Madhouse was producing, but he'd been impressed with Hosoda's *Digimon* films; when Maruyama asked if he would be interested in working with the director, he immediately agreed.

"I met Hosoda in February 2004. My first impression was he was a unique individual," Saito says. "As soon as we met, he bombarded me with questions: 'Why are you in this industry? Why do you want to make movies?' I thought he was certainly a unique person, but at the same time, the questions he asked were very pure and honest. I felt his passion and resolve as a director and creator. I believe it is vital for the director and the producer to work in lockstep.

"Hosoda had to do *Samurai Champloo* under one of his pseudonyms, Katsuyo Hashimoto," Saito concludes. "A few projects he'd worked on outside of Toei had gained a certain notoriety. There was chatter in the industry about this young, up-and-coming, edgy director. It was actually Hosoda, but people were talking about Katsuyo Hashimoto."

OPPOSITE **Three stills from the opening scenes of Shinichiro Watanabe's *Samurai Champloo*, which Hosoda directed, introduce the main characters. Top to bottom: Jin, the icy, honorable ronin; Fuu, the clumsy waitress on a quest; Mugen, the outrageous brawler..**

時をかける少女

II.
THE GIRL WHO LEAPT THROUGH TIME

I ran *The Girl Who Leapt Through Time* by Toei, and they rejected it unanimously, but I thought it had some potential. When I presented it to Masao Maruyama, he immediately said, "That's it!" I could finally see the light at the end of the tunnel. To come through this challenge and have Maruyama say, "That's it!" gave me a new hope to be able to make movies.

—MAMORU HOSODA

After Hosoda left Studio Ghibli, Hayao Miyazaki directed

Howl's Moving Castle. "Coming off *Howl* and going back to Toei was a very painful experience," Hosoda recalls. "That a project could be greenlit and not be finished was a huge failure in my mind. But there was a part of me that still wanted to make movies: If a bus hit me the next day and I died, I didn't think I could allow myself to die without having made some kind of feature film.

"Some of my colleagues told me when I returned, 'If you had quit Toei to make that movie, it could have succeeded. You didn't show enough resolve,'" he continues. "It was a hard thing to swallow, but there was probably some truth to it, which is why I wanted the opportunity for a revenge match, if you want to call it that: creating *The Girl Who Leapt Through Time*."

Back at Toei, Hosoda worked on the television series *Magical Doremi Dokkān*. A number of older viewers commented, "This is like Hosoda's take on *The Girl Who Leapt Through Time*."

Hosoda initially pitched the idea of *The Girl Who Leapt Through Time* at Toei: The studio was celebrating its fiftieth anniversary, and there was talk about making one or more features to mark the occasion. Although he presented several ideas, none of them were greenlit. In retrospect, Hosoda feels the Toei management wasn't serious about the initiative.

Looking back on that early point in their friendship and professional relationship, Saito recalls, "When *Howl's Moving Castle* didn't go well, Hosoda was slightly ostracized in the industry. You could tell there was a little distance between him and a lot of the other creators. He was working on *Magical Doremi Dokkān*, but Masao Maruyama [the co-founder of Madhouse] said, 'You should be making movies; this isn't your wheelhouse.' Hosoda was a director on salary at Toei, so leaving would be a big leap. But Maruyama almost threatened him, saying, 'If you're going to direct movies, you really have to devote yourself to that wholeheartedly.'"

Yasutaka Tsutsui's fantasy novel *The Girl Who Leapt Through Time* first appeared in book form in 1967 and was an immediate hit. By the time Hosoda began work on his version, it had already been adapted for television four times as well as made into two feature films and a manga. (Another TV show, a live-action film, and a stage play would follow Hosoda's version.) The first feature adaptation, directed by Nobuhiko Obayashi and starring actress/singer Tomoyo Harada, had been the second-highest-grossing film in Japan in 1983.

"In my first year of middle school, I read *The Girl Who Leapt Through Time*, but I didn't see the film when it came out in the summer of '83," Hosoda confesses. "That was my first year of high school—my rebellious years, when everything was stinky and gross. Later, I watched a rental tape, but couldn't accept it. Several years later, I re-watched it and, embarrassingly, concluded it's a masterpiece."

PREVIOUS SPREAD **Makoto's initial accident triggers her ability to time leap.**

OPPOSITE **Makoto lands amid the trash cans at her school after a time leap.**

真琴 MAKOTO

紺野真琴①

下着見せないように
時にはスカートが少し
長めになったり…

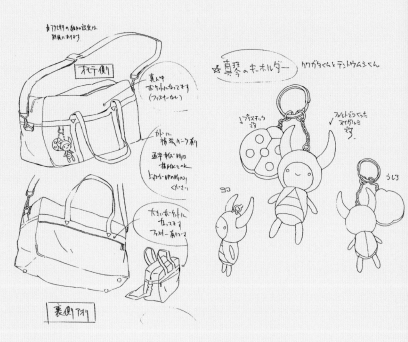

真琴の自転車改の改

＊キャラは対比のみの参考です

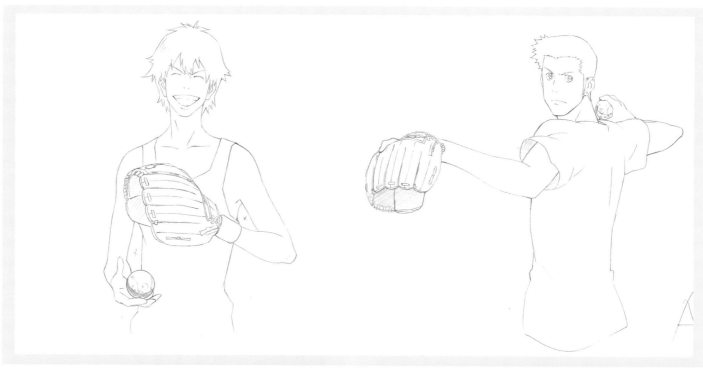

OPPOSITE **A model sheet of Makoto shows her attitude, costume, and expressions.**

ABOVE **The informal baseball games the friends play showcase the personalities of the irreverent Chiaki (LEFT) and the serious Kosuke. Animation drawings and final frames.**

FOLLOWING SPREAD **Model sheets for Makoto's best friends: Chiaki's bad posture, shaggy hair, and untidy clothes provide a visual contrast to the fastidious Kosuke.**

Working with veteran screenwriter Satoko Okudera, Hosoda expanded and deepened the original fantasy. They kept the focus on three high school friends who hang out together, but added their low-key baseball games to provide visual interest, instead of just showing the characters sitting around talking. "*The Girl Who Leapt Through Time* had been adapted before, but each time they'd taken a very serious approach," Hosoda recalls. "I wanted it to be something a younger audience could enjoy. It wasn't as much about nostalgia as it was about thoroughly enjoying this experience. I wanted to turn the idea of time travel into a comedic element, which really translated to the karaoke scene. My foremost objective was to make it a really, really fun movie."

Hosoda and Okudera began their transformation of the story by making the characters more multilayered, contemporary, and appealing. Tsutsui's Goro, a fussy shopkeeper's son, became Kosuke, the diligent son of a doctor. Kazuo, who remains a rather vague character in the book, was transformed into the irreverent Chiaki. At the center of the story, Kazuko was reimagined as the less bossy but more dimensional Makoto—the first of Hosoda's complex heroines. The utter, quotidian normalcy of three friends who bat flies, play catch, and talk makes Makoto's ability to manipulate time seem all the more fantastic.

David Silverman, the Oscar-nominated director of the *Simpsons* short "The Longest Day Care" and *The Simpsons Movie*, comments, "I've never seen anyone depict young adults so realistically: friendship, slight flirting,

千昭 CHIAKI

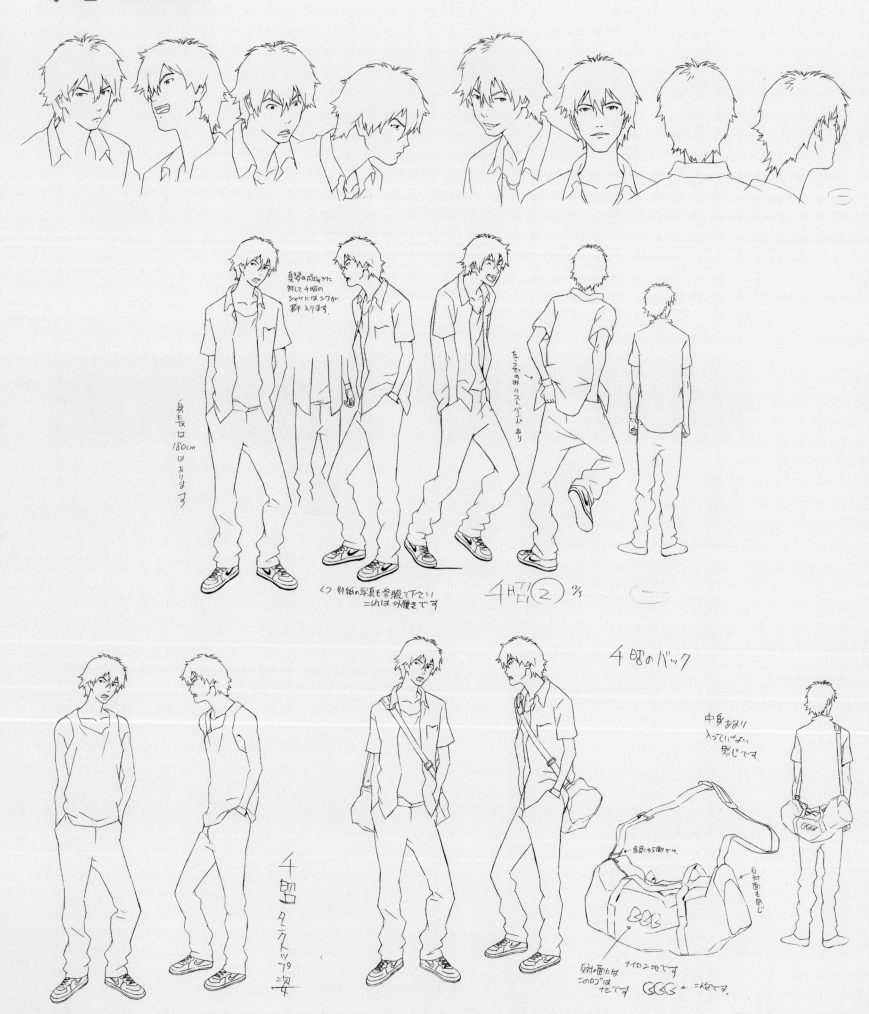

功介 KOSUKE

*くつ、別紙写真も参照して下さい
これは外履きです

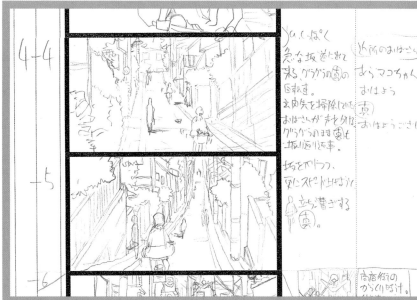

talking about relationships. Very subtle, nothing overwrought, nothing over-dramatic, nothing romanticized. Just a clear way of showing how humans behave that's really smart, really subtle, very funny, and very engaging."

The designs for the characters reflected Hosoda's revisions of their personalities: Short, stocky, red-faced Goro was transformed into tall, hand-some Kosuke. Chiaki is also tall, but shaggy and untidy in contrast to his serious friend Kosuke. Makoto is cute enough to make the boys' attraction to her credible, but there's a slightly clumsy quality to her movements, as she often fails to pay attention to what's going on around her.

Animator and animation director Hiroyuki Aoyama, who had met Hosoda on the *One Piece* movie and would work on all his subsequent films, says, "I began on *The Girl Who Leapt Through Time* as a key animator, and was put into position of animation director. There were three of us working in that position, and as the project progressed, I found myself doing some character design. I had to change about 80 percent of the character designs that we had received. Looking back, I would say there are many scenes I wish I could have done more on as animation director, but given the many hats I had to wear, I wasn't able to."

Hosoda's first personal film, *The Girl Who Leapt Through Time*, already showed his rare ability to create characters who are credible, likable individuals. "Hosoda isn't dealing with princesses or superheroes, but with characters who are just everyday. It's not easy to create that kind of character," says *Beauty and the Beast* producer Don Hahn. "There are very few animated movies from the last five or ten years that are memorable because a character really pops out as a flesh and blood human being. In animation, it's too easy to not just caricature but make it bland; Hosoda doesn't. He'll take a girl and make her very, very normal. You not only know that girl on the screen, but you have a sense of what she's like off the screen, too."

Makoto's first time leap is much scarier than her rather mild experience in the book. She has to run an errand for her mother, delivering some peaches to a family friend known as Auntie Witch. The viewer gets the feeling she's bicycled along these streets countless times—the scenery is so familiar, it doesn't register. When an elaborate set of clockwork gnomes atop a department store begin to strike the hour, Makoto doesn't even look up. But when she reaches the steep hill that slopes down to the train crossing, her brakes fail. She tries dragging her feet; one shoe flies off. As the hour strikes with a resonant tone, she hits the pedestrian gate and is

TOP LEFT **Hosoda scouting a location for** *The Girl Who Leapt Through Time*

ABOVE **Two storyboard panels and final frames show Makoto cycling through her hilly neighborhood.**

OPPOSITE **A background painting of the hillside where the key action in the film occurs**

thrown into the air in front of the oncoming train. Then suddenly, she's back up the hill, disentangling herself and her bike from an irate woman she's run into.

She describes her frightening encounter to Auntie Witch, an art conservator, who explains that Makoto has leapt through time, and that many young women experience the same phenomenon. She shrugs off the near-death experience as if it were no more remarkable than doing well on a test or finding a becoming sweater.

Makoto eagerly experiments with her newfound ability. A flying leap and a focus on jumping through time is all it takes: A shift occurs and she rolls back into the scene. She begins using the time leap as a "replay" button on her life. She extends a karaoke session with Kosuke and Chiaki for ten hours and comes home hoarse. She retakes a quiz she flunked and aces it, as she already knows the questions. She manipulates another student into causing an accidental fire while making tempura in cooking class, and she tries to arrange for her shy classmate Kaho to confess her love for Kosuke. Although she's attracted to Chiaki, she repeatedly avoids opportunities for him to ask her out.

"Hosoda has a command of action, not only of action performance but also action cutting," adds Silverman. "That hit me in *The Girl Who Leapt Through Time*, when the time leaps occur. Not just the very dramatic one, where it looks like she's going to get hit

ABOVE **Makoto has an accident in cooking class** (LEFT), **then uses a time leap to make another student cause the accident— which spirals out of control** (RIGHT).

OPPOSITE **Hosoda's storyboard shows some of the accidents Makoto tries to avoid through time leaps.**

No. 29

S	C	画　面

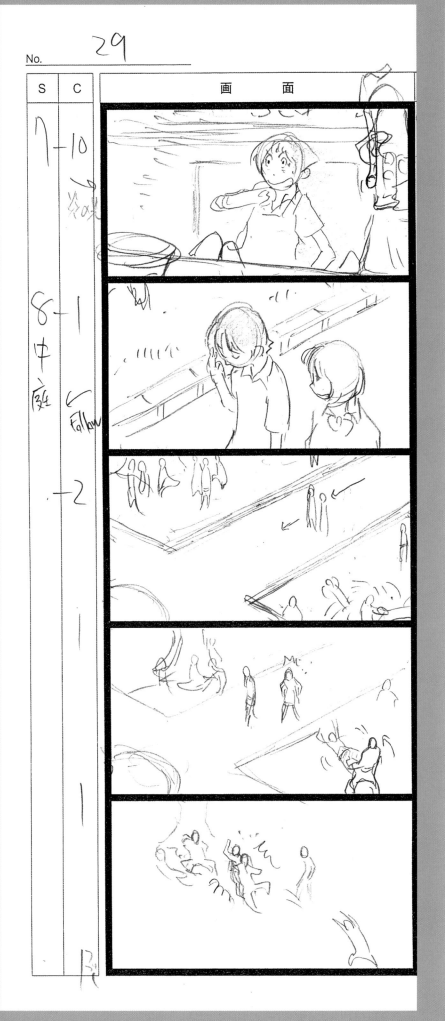

No. 135

S	C	画　面

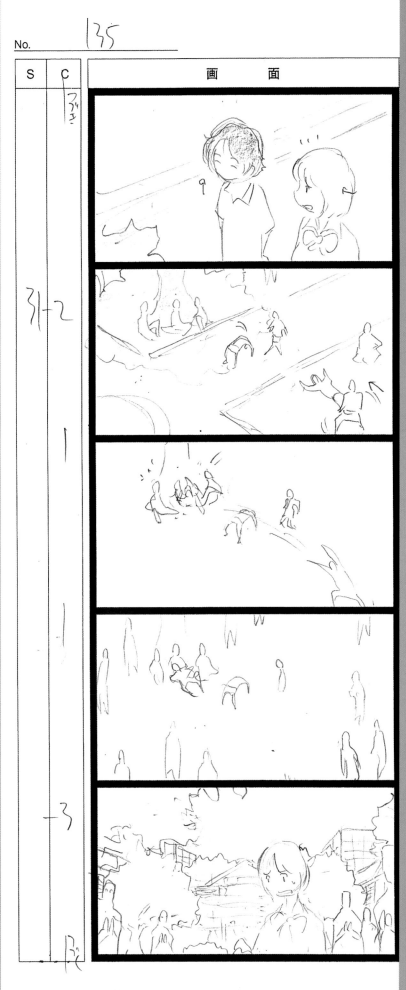

29

THIS PAGE In Hosoda's storyboards, Makoto makes three leaps—and three clumsy landings.

OPPOSITE Jaw set, Makoto launches herself into the unknown in a series of animation drawings with frames from the same sequence. Different colored pages indicate which artist made the drawing: The director's fixes are on blue paper; the assistant director's, pink; the director of animation's, green; the lead animator's, yellow. The *genga*, or original key animation drawings, are on white paper.

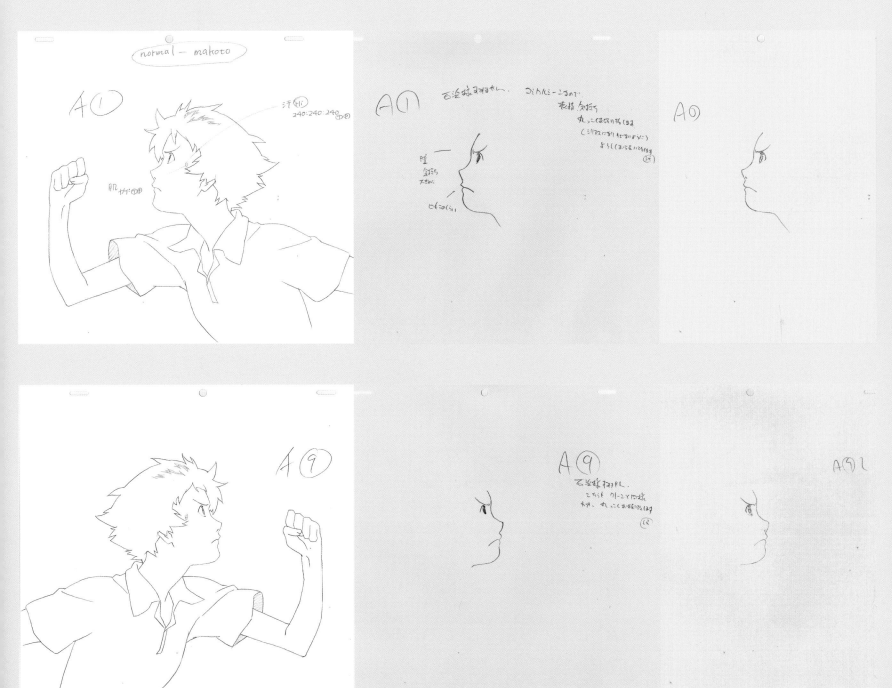

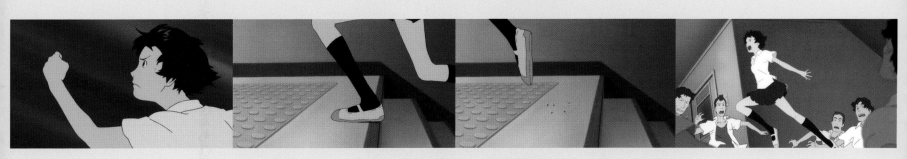

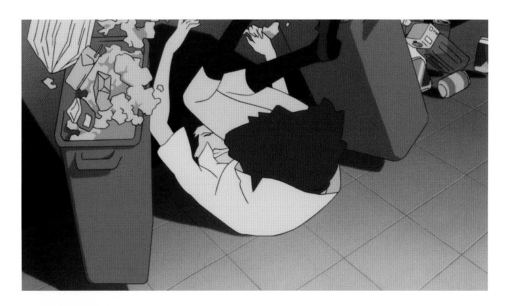

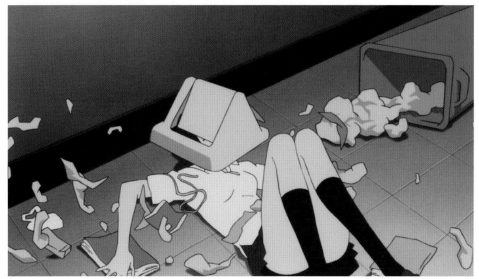

OPPOSITE **School trash cans provide a less than ideal landing pad in this sequence of animation drawings.**

RIGHT **Makoto lands with more force than grace in the finished film.**

by the train—that's a focal point in the film, which is great. But especially her comedic crashes, when she lands in the room where they're singing karaoke, or at school when she keeps banging into filing cabinets like a bowling ball crashing into the pins. The shorthand is clear: 'That didn't work. Let's try this one.'"

"It was fun to use repetition in the editing as a tool, but there is always an underlying purpose behind it," Hosoda explains. "When Okudera and I talked about that approach, we watched *Groundhog Day* and thought it offered a good merger of repetition and comedy. The idea of repeating something over and over has a naturally movie-like quality. Adding time travel to the repetitions made for a very good, synergistic narrative tool."

"When you use the same cut in the same tempo, you create a certain rhythm," observes Shigeru Nishiyama, who has edited all of Hosoda's personal films. "In some scenes, we shifted away from that by altering the time to build some tension."

Makoto learns the unhappy lesson that altering the past can have unexpected and even dangerous consequences. The boy who caused the fire in cooking class gets into

fights with other students over the incident and accidentally injures a bystander. Kaho endures mortifying embarassment when she tries to confess to Kosuke. Makoto suffers pangs of jealousy when the frustrated Chiaki asks another girl out.

As she hurtles up a staircase, preparing to leap yet again, Makoto overhears a piano student playing Bach's *Goldberg Variations*, which consists of an aria followed by a series of thirty variations and a recapitulation—an apt parallel to what Makoto is experiencing.

Hosoda increased the number of time leaps from the novel and altered Makoto's reasons for them, just as he changed the characters' personalities. "As I was developing *Girl*, it became quite different from the original work, but Tsutsui thought that was a good thing," Hosoda says. "He felt that strictly adhering to the original was not necessarily what a movie adaptation needed. A lot of authors would say, 'You've deviated from the story. How could you?' Tsutsui was very understanding and open."

At the climax of the film, Kosuke takes Kaho on Makoto's bicycle to see his physician father. The brakes fail on the steep hill, and the initial accident recurs. Kosuke tries to skid to a stop and his shoe flies off; the gnomes on the

clock perform their little dance; the hour strikes; the note sounds, the bicycle hits the barrier; and both students are thrown into the air in front of the oncoming train.

The audience recognizes the scene Makoto experienced, but Hosoda once again varies the details just enough to create a disquieting uncertainty. "The first time he cuts back to the little automatons on the sign, I thought, *Oh, that again*," says Silverman. "But each time, it's a little different. The first time they're charming, but they become more and more ominous."

Time somehow stops. Kosuke and Kaho hang in midair as Chiaki appears and asks Makoto about her time-leaping. Like Kazuo in the novel, he is from the future and understands the phenomenon better than Makoto—or Auntie Witch. He undoes the accident, warning Makoto that in one version of events, her two friends were killed.

Tsutsui's Kazuo is an advanced chemistry student from the twenty-seventh century who was testing an experimental compound that enabled him to teleport freely at will. His experiment backfired, and he found himself trapped in the twentieth century, where he discovered the pleasures of friendship and baseball—and fell in love with Kazuko. Having re-created his elixir with its signature scent of lavender, he's preparing to leave and must erase everyone's memories of him.

Chiaki came back to the twentieth century to see a painting that no longer exists in his time: *A Picture of White Plum and Camellia and Chrysanthemum*—the same painting Makoto sees Auntie Witch conserving for the museum where she works. He also enjoyed his agreeably ordinary life in suburban Tokyo, and fell in love.

As he leaves, Tsutsui's Kazuo tells Kazuko he will return someday with a different identity to visit her. Hosoda's Chiaki warns Makoto to be more careful and less clumsy, lest she hurt herself or one of her friends. Heartbroken that those are his last words to her, she bursts into tears. Chiaki reappears, touches her hair, and reassures her he will be waiting for her in the future.

"In the film directed by Obayashi, the environment had been destroyed in the future world, and the boy visits the present to collect plants that have become extinct," Hosoda explains. "His purpose reflected the social issues of that time. I wanted the purpose for the boy's travel to the present to be different. I thought it would be for some spiritual reason, rather than to pick up something material."

The painting Chiaki wants to see is housed in a museum copied from the Tokyo National Museum in Ueno Park. As part of his research, Hosoda met with an old friend from Kanazawa College of Art, Masato Matsushima—now a curator at the museum. Hosoda initially felt jealous that Matsushima worked in a "wonderful place" where he could research works of art to his heart's content.

"While I did not know the specifics of the film Hosoda was making, I asked if the film could be set here, to interest more people in the museum," Matsushima explains. "I thought it would be nice to curate an exhibition in the main

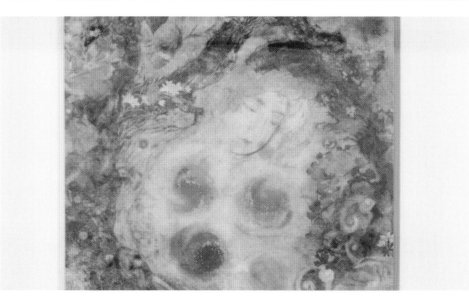

OPPOSITE **A background painting of the museum where Makoto visits Auntie Witch**

TOP **The interior of the museum was inspired by the Tokyo National Museum in Ueno Park.**

ABOVE RIGHT **Makoto and Auntie Witch view the art on display in the museum.**

RIGHT *White Plum Tree, Camellia and Chrysanthemum*: **The painting Chiaki came to the twenty-first century to see. Artist: Toshio Hirata**

building. Although only a few items can be visibly identified in the film, I selected about twenty works to fit in the space. While it's a fictional exhibition, the biggest challenge was the director's request to select anonymous works, because the interpretation of an image would be limited by the name of a well-known painter."

Hosoda and Matsushima agreed everything in the exhibit would be by Japanese artists, but the key work would be the imaginary *A Picture of White Plum and Camellia and Chrysanthemum*." Hosoda felt Chiaki's interest in the art should be based on totally different values from a spectator in the present, just as a foreigner would perceive Japanese art differently from someone with a knowledge of Japanese culture.

Complementing the accurately rendered interiors of the museum are the lush watercolor exterior backgrounds, which suggest the crushing heat and humidity of the Japanese summer. In the *Boston Globe*, critic Ty Burr praised *The Girl Who Leapt Through Time*: "White cumulus clouds pile up in the backgrounds of scenes, and the buzz of locusts drifts through the humid air, intertwining with sleepy Bach preludes [*sic*] on the soundtrack. Director Mamoru Hosoda roots the story in a specific neighborhood at a specific season before he starts uprooting his heroine's sense of time. Instead of the usual manic anime approach, the film is rich and observant."

Hosoda uses the massive clouds, huge trees, whining cicadas, and tinkling glass wind chimes as the audiovisual equivalents of a *kisetsu*, the seasonal signifier employed by haiku poets to anchor their verses in a specific moment. He would use similar effects in *Summer Wars*, *Wolf Children*, and *Mirai*.

As the film neared completion, Hosoda discovered that although Toei usually opened their films in 250 theaters, the distributor, Kadokawa Herald Pictures, planned to give *The Girl Who Leapt Through Time* a very limited release. "It was going to be rolled out in six theaters in all of Japan," he says. "When I heard that I thought, *Well, my career is over.*

Producing a $2 million-plus movie and screening it in six theaters would make it impossible to achieve any kind of commercial success—or even recoup its costs. I was never going to get the chance to make a movie again, so I was determined to leave nothing on the table."

Although *The Girl Who Leapt Through Time* opened in only a few theaters and had a limited advertising budget, the film received good reviews and benefited from enthusiastic word of mouth. In Shinjuku, the film played to standing-room audiences. *When The Girl Who Leapt Through Time* ran for more than forty weeks, the distributor expanded the release to more than one hundred theaters and submittedthe film to international festivals.

At the Tokyo International Anime Fair in March 2006, Tsutsui praised the film as "a true second-generation" of his novel. *The Girl Who Leapt Through Time* won the Best Animation Film award from both the Japanese Academy and the Mainichi Film Concours. It swept the Tokyo Anime Awards, winning Animation of the Year, Best Art Direction, Best Character Design, Best Director, Best Original Story, and Best Screenplay.

Overseas, it won Best Animation Film at the Sitges Festival and a Special Distinction prize at the 2007 Annecy Animation Festival. In the *Guardian*, Phelim O'Neill wrote, "The characters are entirely credible and likable, the simply drawn figures highly effective against the lush background artwork. Time travel has rarely seemed so joyous." David Jenkins in *Time Out* said, "Superior anime caper comedy with wit, energy, and mad invention to spare."

Looking back, Hosoda reflects, "Regardless of the initial commercial success, I think the overwhelming support from the fans allowed me to make more movies—and to continue making movies to this day. I was surprised when *The Girl Who Leapt Through Time* began picking up traction in foreign film festivals, starting with Annecy. I wrote a story about this average girl who lives on the outskirts of Tokyo; that it had any worldwide appeal was kind of mind-boggling."

LEFT **Hosoda with the Special Distinction Trophy at the 2007 Annecy International Animated Film Festival**

OPPOSITE, TOP **A background painting of Makoto's house and overgrown garden**

OPPOSITE, BOTTOM **The baseball diamond where Makoto and her friends hang out**

FRIENDSHIP:
BASEBALL & KARAOKE

The informal baseball games are an essential part of the friendship Makoto, Chiaki, and Kosuke share.

RIGHT Hosoda's storyboards of a conversation held during a game of catch

BELOW Frames of the game

OPPOSITE Makoto stretches a karaoke session over several hours in storyboards and final frames.

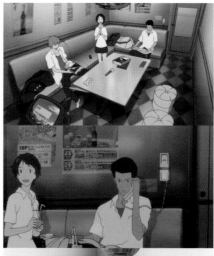

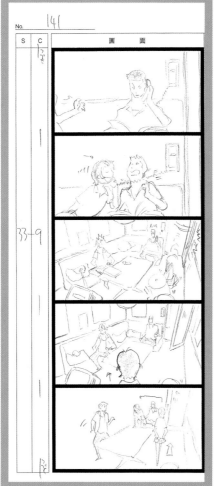

小物 SMALL ARTICLES

Hosoda believes that in an animated film, characters' homes reveal details about their personalities that audiences would take for granted in a live-action film.

BELOW Storyboards of Makoto and her sister in the bedroom they share

BOTTOM The toys and products in the girls' bedroom suggests their tastes, including a fondness for *kawaii,* or "ultra-cute," plush figures.

OPPOSITE, TOP An art setting of the room includes a note about an anthropomorphized tissue box.

OPPOSITE, MIDDLE A preliminary painting of the shared bedroom

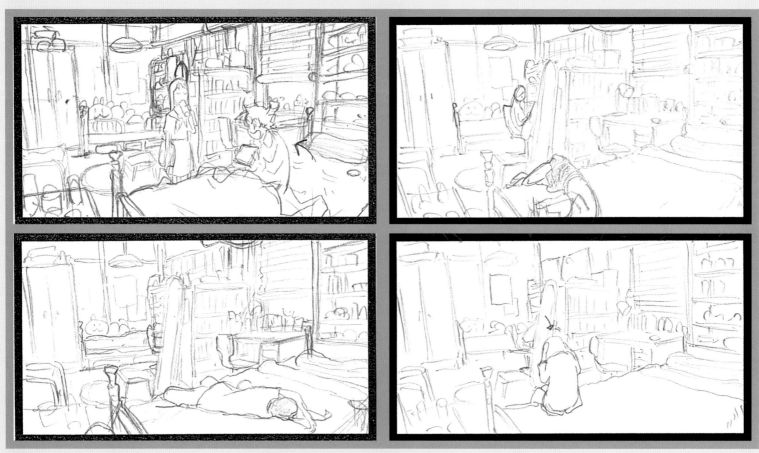

真琴の部屋のぬいぐるみ Makoto's plush toys

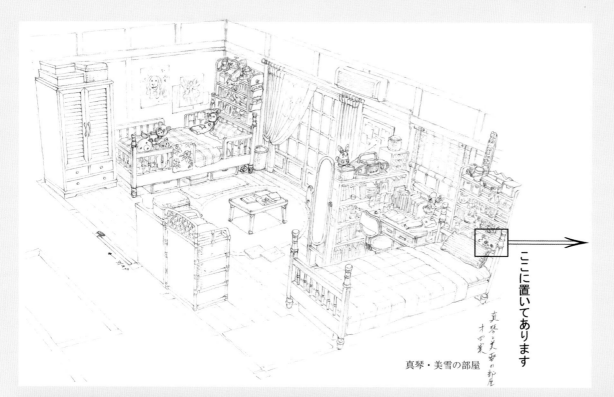

真琴のティッシュ箱 Makoto's tissue box

ここに置いてあります

真琴・美雪の部屋

BELOW Two frames from the film: The background artists have filled with toys the shelves over Makoto's bed.

THE FIRST ACCIDENT

Frames from the film echo Hosoda's storyboards, which set the sequence of events and recurring images (like the clockwork musicians) in the first, near-fatal accident that initially propels Makoto through time.

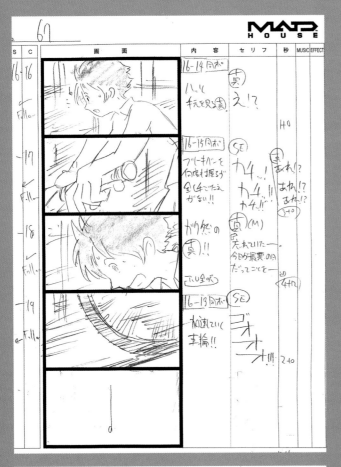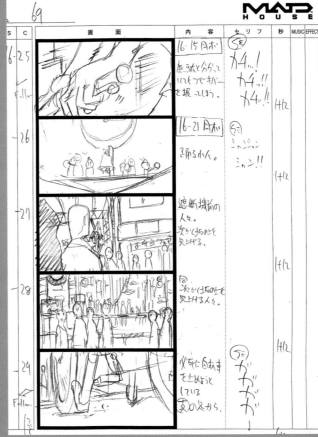

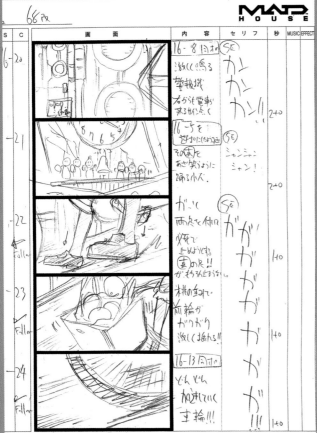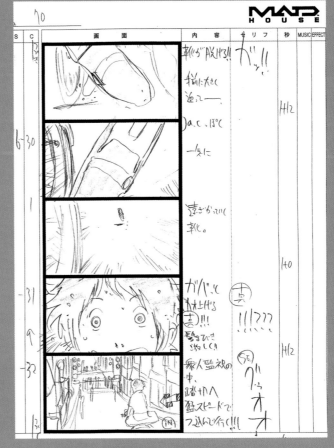

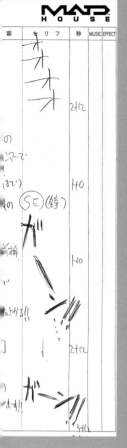
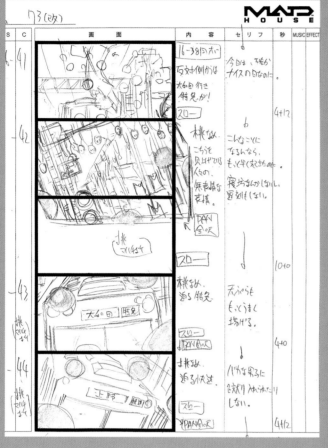
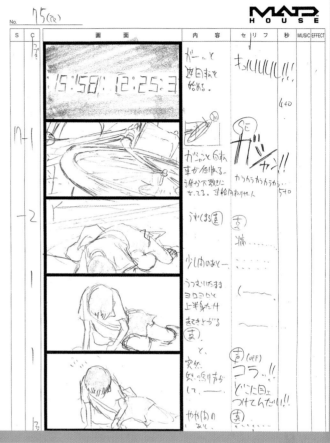

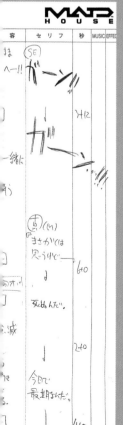
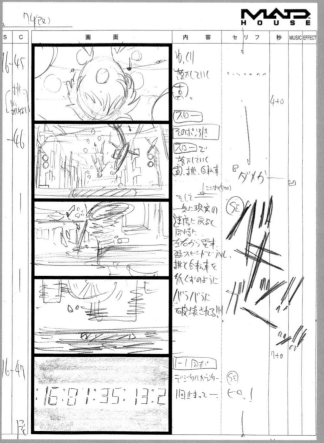
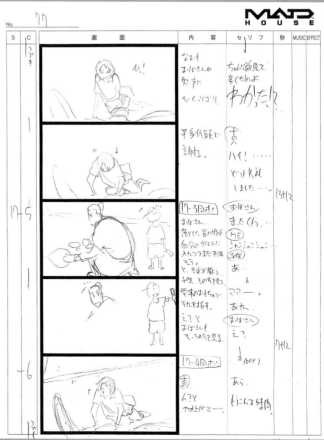

THE SECOND ACCIDENT

Storyboards and stills show Hosoda uses similar but not identical images in the second accident to create tension. The audience recognizes the menace of the situation, but nothing is exactly the same.

Chiaki uses his superior knowledge and power to undo Makoto's mistakes. At the end of the film, he assures her he will be waiting for her—in the future.

OPPOSITE Chiaki bids farewell to Makoto in the storyboards and the final film.

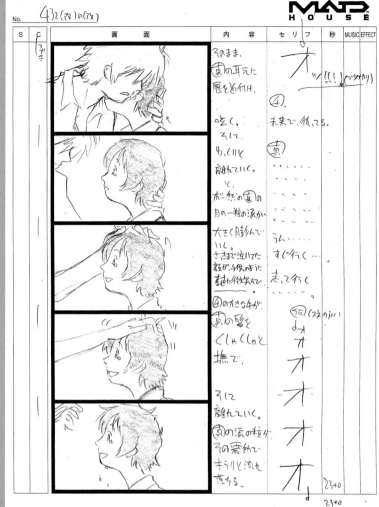

時をかける少女

2006 SUMMER ROADSHOW

MARKETING

Some of the merchandise tied to the film, including (CLOCKWISE FROM RIGHT) a magnet, jewelry, cork sticker, smartphone case, a pen and notebook, hair tie, and mug

OPPOSITE The poster for *The Girl Who Leapt Through Time*. The image of Makoto leaping would later become the logo of Studio Chizu (THIS PAGE, BELOW).

STUDIO CHIZU

Magnet

時をかける少女
THE GIRL WHO LEAPT THROUGH TIME

Time waits for no one.

時をかける少女
THE GIRL WHO LEAPT THROUGH TIME

thermo mug

THE GIRL
WHO LEAPT THROUGH TIME

NOTEBOOK

THE GIRL WHO LEAPT THROUGH TIME

THE GIRL
WHO LEAPT
THROUGH TIME

III.

サマーウォーズ

SUMMER
WARS

Hosoda's previous films had been based on extant

properties (*Digimon* and *One Piece*) or novels (*The Girl Who Leapt Through Time* and the never-completed version of *Howl's Moving Castle*). *Summer Wars* was an original story conceived by Hosoda; Satoko Okudera wrote the screenplay. "The biggest influence for the idea was the new circumstances surrounding me," he says. "I got married and welcomed into a big new family. Having complete strangers become relatives was a fascinating experience that inspired me while making the movie."

"Until Hosoda married, he didn't have a large extended family. His mother was the only blood relative still in his life; one of the older ladies in *Summer Wars* was inspired by her," producer Yuichiro Saito explains. "Through marriage, he was able to discover what a family is. He wanted to show his mom he was making family movies; unfortunately, two months before the film was completed, she passed away."

Although they originally planned to market the film primarily to an audience of Japanese animation fans, its focus shifted as Hosoda considered his experiences at international animation festivals. "They're gatherings of directors from around the world who exchange ideas that are culturally relevant at the time," he explains. "The films I saw were generally

I wanted all the characters to be realistic: There are no superheroes or mecha in real life. I wanted to make an action film in which a crisis arises and people solve it in today's Japanese society.

—MAMORU HOSODA

PREVIOUS SPREAD **The rogue AI program Love Machine battles King Kazma, martial arts champion of OZ.**

ABOVE **Two animation drawings from the previous scene**

very family-oriented, but there wasn't anything showing a Japanese family to the world. That was the inception of *Summer War*s. I wasn't out to make a blockbuster summer hit. I wanted to depict a Japanese family head-on and create something that we could talk about."

As the film opens, high school nerd Kenji Koiso laments he was only a runner-up for the Japanese Math Olympics team. He ruefully notes that it's fortunate he's good at math, "because I suck at everything else." Kenji plans to spend the summer working as a part-time "code monkey," doing routine maintenance for the global computer network OZ.

OZ suggests an all-encompassing amalgamation of Twitter, Facebook, Google, and Amazon—without the real-world product placement of *Ralph Breaks the Internet*. The Grid in *TRON: Legacy* is a grim wasteland; the cyber world in *Ready Player One* is more crowded but also dark. OZ boasts gleaming white surfaces and attractions rendered in brilliant DayGlo™ pastels.

The filmmakers envisioned people from all over the planet constantly linked to OZ through their computers, game stations, tablets, and cell phones to chat with friends, pay bills, telecommute, monitor medical data, and engage in cyber sports. To make OZ feel accessible to everyone, not just *otaku* (rabid fans of anime, manga, and other aspects of

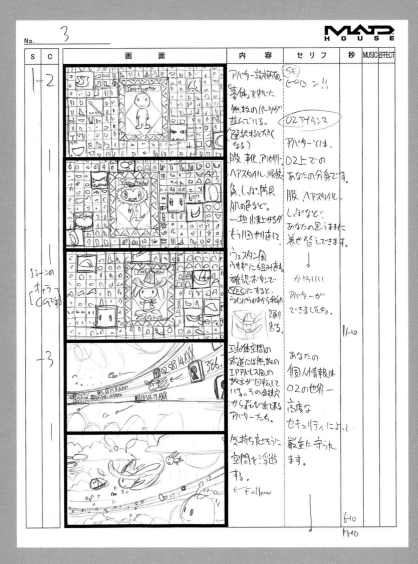

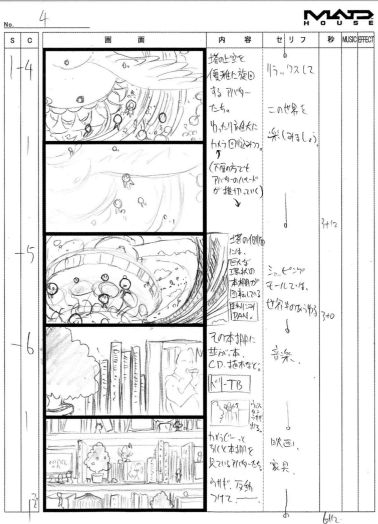

pop culture), the designers made the personal avatars cute and colorful.

Many journalists tied the look of OZ to the Louis Vuitton promotional film, but Hosoda traces it back further. "When Louis Vuitton approached us, I heard they said, 'We want to work with this Mamoru Hosoda,'" he recalls. "That was flattering, but when I looked at their presentation, I could see that the digital world we'd created in *Digimon Adventure: Our War Game!* was the look they were going for: a clean, white slate with bursts of color here and there. Journalists ask me all the time, 'Did you get the look of *Summer Wars* from the Louis Vuitton monogram?'—but *Digimon* actually precedes it."

"When we were trying to create a visual representation of the cyber world, Hosoda wanted a ring or equator-like line that would run around the circumference of that world," explains production designer Anri Jojo. "From there, we were able to see the scope of the world, and slowly worked our way in toward the center. I made several design suggestions but couldn't get Hosoda to say 'OK' to any of them. Finally, he said, 'I want it to have a face.' I responded with the totem pole–like design, with faces stacked one on top of another, and he signed off on it."

Although cell phones, online games, and the Web have become standard elements in anime series and films, Hosoda captures the importance of social networking and the constant presence of the Internet in contemporary life. For Kenji and the other characters, OZ is as much a part of everyday life as the real world.

Hosoda and his artists present a striking visual contrast between the cool, hallucinatory realm of OZ and the oppressive heat of a Japanese summer in his wife's native Nagano Prefecture. The real world is depicted via watercolor backgrounds that feel even more atmospheric than the ones in *The Girl Who Leapt Through Time*. Yoji Takeshige, who had worked as art director on many of the Studio Ghibli films, including *Spirited Away*, *My Neighbors the Yamadas*, and Miyazaki's version of *Howl's Moving Castle*, did key work

OPPOSITE The rounded shapes and bright pastels of OZ are designed to feel welcoming to users of all ages, genders, levels of education, etc.

LEFT Hosoda's storyboards show how users would be welcomed to the cyber realm of OZ with the creation of an avatar.

on the visuals of the natural world of Nagano. "I thought for the film, the background art would be a very effective way to describe the heat and humidity of a Japanese summer: wide, blue skies and green mountains," says Hosoda. "Art director Yôji Takeshige draws beautiful nature scenes, and his talent played a great role."

Paul Felix, production designer of Disney's *Big Hero 6*, comments, "I love the contrast between the fully realized three-dimensional paintings of the real world and the implied space of OZ. Space seems much more abstract in OZ, and it has an almost adolescent sense of color, which makes it feel like something's wrong with it. When Love Machine's attacks occur, that palette makes it seem even more sinister."

Kenji is ecstatic when he's offered a job by Natsuki Shinohara, whom he regards as the most attractive girl in their school. Too late, he discovers she wants him to pose as her fiancé at her great-grandmother's nineti-eth birthday celebration. He's thrust into Natsuki's large, fractious family, who squabble and cite their exalted Jinnouchi samurai clan ancestors at every meal. They initially dismiss Kenji when they discover he isn't an honors student at prestigious Tokyo University or the scion of a great old family, as Natsuki had claimed. But they soon become fond of him and protect him from the police when he's wrongly accused of breaking OZ's security system.

Kenji Koiso and his friend Takashi Sakuma perform routine mainte-nance on OZ in their clubroom and as avatars in the cyber world: "a couple of part-time code monkeys."

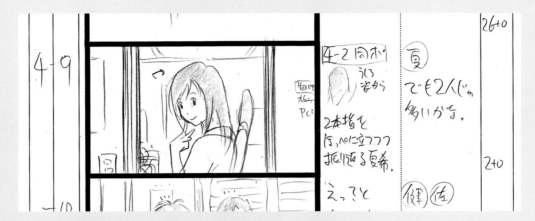

Natsuki needs someone for "a part-time job."

ABOVE Hosoda's storyboard panel sets her pose.

RIGHT The colored image of Natsuki over the layout drawing for the scene

BELOW The final image of Natsuki over the finished background

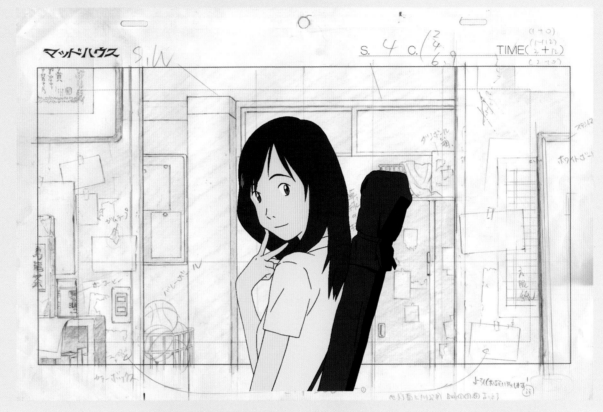

ABOVE LEFT Kenji awkwardly attempts to chat with Natsuki's formidable great-grandmother Sakae.

ABOVE Sakae's stern visage over a layout drawing of the view from her window

LEFT The Jinnouchi family at dinner. Kenji, who lives alone with his working mother, has never experienced such a large, intense family gathering.

Great-grandmother Sakae immediately recognizes the strength and kindness hiding beneath Kenji's insecure exterior. She's moved when Kenji thanks her for her hospitality, noting that he'd never had the chance "to eat together like a family" with so many people. Her affection for Kenji is no small distinction: When this formidable matriarch gets mad at her ne'er-do-well adopted son Wabisuke, she grabs the *naginata* from an antique suit of armor and threatens to skewer him.

"Sakae's character was influenced by a lot of people I know, including my own mother and my grandmother," Hosoda says. "Her character also reflects a kind of idealized view we Japanese have toward our mothers and grandmothers."

Like Makoto and her friends in *The Girl Who Leapt Through Time*, the characters in *Summer Wars* are multidimensional. They have faults. Natsuki is not an idealized princess longing for a prince, and no one would mistake Kenji for Prince Charming. *Summer Wars* deals with tradition and respect among generations.

The Jinnouchi clan has to stop bullying Kenji when a rogue artificial intelligence program known as Love Machine attacks OZ. At first, everyone believes Kenji gave the monster access to the system by solving a complex

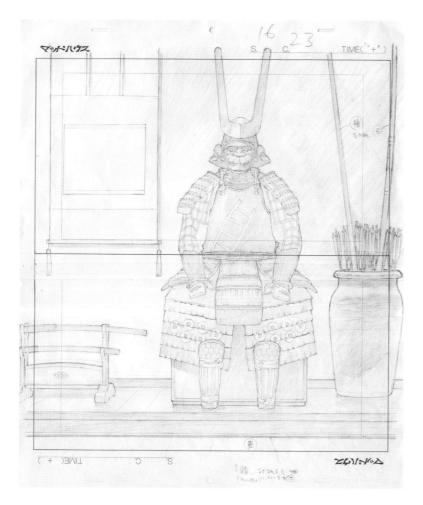

TOP LEFT A layout drawing of the interior of the Jinnouchi home, showing armor and weapons used by their samurai ancestors in the late sixteenth century

TOP RIGHT The finished background painting

ABOVE When Sakae grows angry at her adopted son Wabisuke, she menaces him with a *naginata,* a halberd-like weapon taken from the display of armor.

RIGHT Kenji focuses on cracking a mathematical puzzle in the battle against Love Machine.

陣内 JINNOUCHI FAMILY TREE

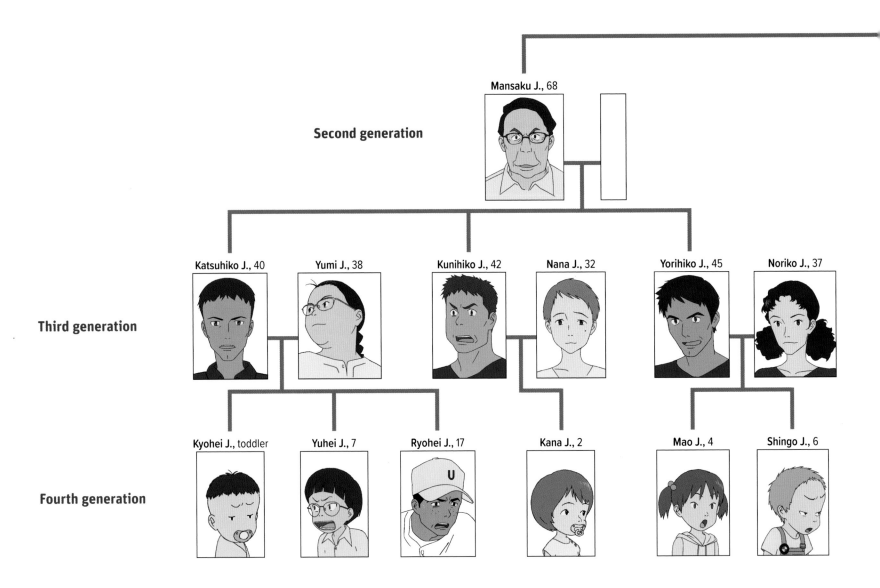

Second generation

Mansaku J., 68

Third generation

Katsuhiko J., 40 | Yumi J., 38 | Kunihiko J., 42 | Nana J., 32 | Yorihiko J., 45 | Noriko J., 37

Fourth generation

Kyohei J., toddler | Yuhei J., 7 | Ryohei J., 17 | Kana J., 2 | Mao J., 4 | Shingo J., 6

Character comparison diagram

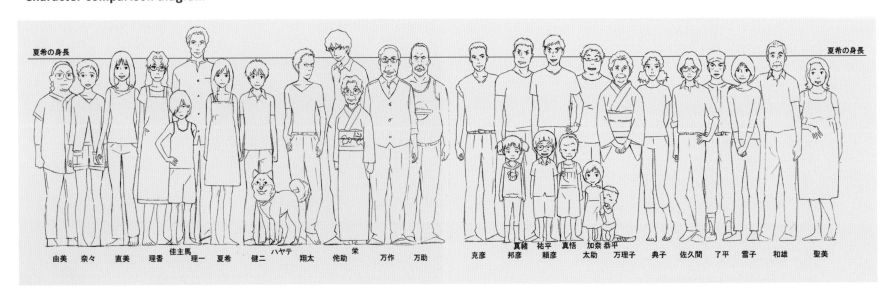

夏希の身長

夏希の身長

由美　奈々　直美　理香　佳主馬　理一　夏希　健二　ハヤテ　翔太　侘助　栄　万作　万助

克彦　真緒 祐平 真悟 加奈 恭平　太助　万理子　典子　佐久間　了平　雷子　和雄　聖美

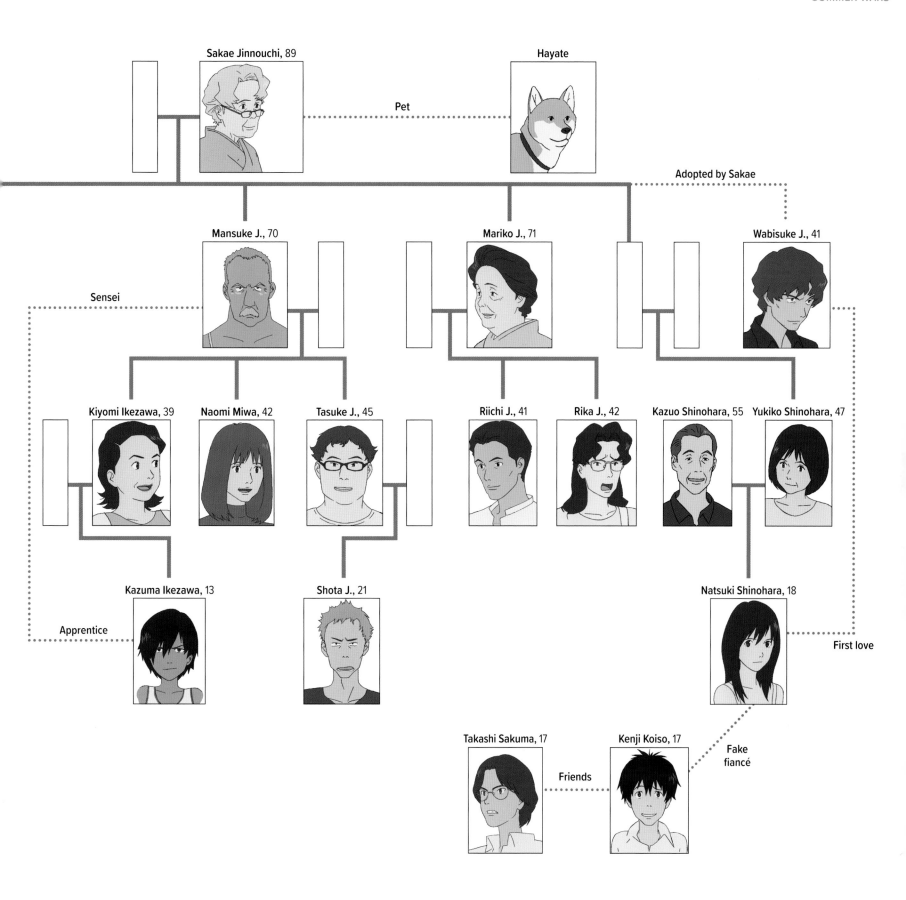

THIS SPREAD **The family tree and size comparison chart of the Jinnouchi clan. As Hosoda notes, it is unusual to have so many individual characters in an animated feature.**

アバター AVATARS

Each avatar in OZ reflects the user's personality, interests, and self- image.

1. Kenji's original avatar suggests a meek boy with outsize, cartoonish ears.

2. When Love Machine absorbs Kenji's avatar, it acquires a malevolent smirk.

3. Takashi provides Kenji with a temporary avatar: a panicky cartoon squirrel.

4–5. Natsuki's original, modest avatar is transformed by John and Yoko, OZ's guardians, into a more powerful image that combines elements of an angel, a phoenix, and a Shinto shrine maiden.

6–9. Many Jinnouchi family members are first responders, and their avatars reflect their professions.

10. Uncle Mansuke, who manages a fishing company, brings cartons of squid to Sakae's ninetieth birthday party.

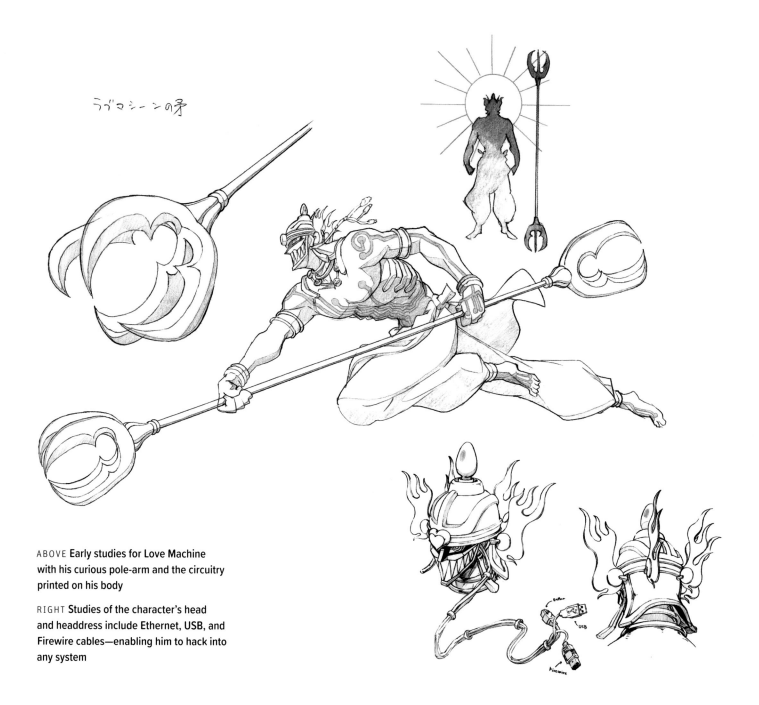

ラブマシーンの矛

ABOVE Early studies for Love Machine with his curious pole-arm and the circuitry printed on his body

RIGHT Studies of the character's head and headdress include Ethernet, USB, and Firewire cables—enabling him to hack into any system

mathematical puzzle that arrived in his email. Solving the puzzle unlocked Oz's top-secret 2,056-digit security code. But Kenji got the last digit wrong: He *didn't* break the Internet. But fifty-five other people correctly solved the puzzle, enabling Love Machine to achieve the hack.

Regardless of who's at fault, the Internet is broken. Nothing works properly; the OZ engineers can't get into the system to repair it; the cheerful white surfaces are defaced with graffiti.

In contrast to the *kawaii* ("ultra-cute") avatars that throng OZ, Love Machine looks like a demon-warrior that might guard the entrance to a Buddhist temple. When it scrambles a wall of panels bearing the names of highways with its polearm, traffic grinds to a halt all over Japan and GPS systems go awry. It pushes over a series of panels that fall like dominos; it yanks down hanging ribbons of symbols; the pressure in city water mains goes haywire; first responders are called to one false alarm after another.

Neither *Ralph Breaks the Internet* nor *Ready Player One* conveys the link between events in the real and cyber worlds as effectively.

Editor Shigeru Nishiyama comments, "It's not so much how the sequence was cut together as much as how the two worlds had been designed to connect with each other. It goes much deeper than just the editing: I would give a lot more credit to the people who came up with the imagery more than the cut itself. I don't want to take too much credit for the linking of the two worlds: That's what makes Hosoda's work so amazing."

"I needed to describe the disorder and destruction of the infrastructure in a simple way, so even little children could follow the story," Hosoda counters. "Anri Jojo, the OZ production designer, gave me lots of ideas to describe those situations visually."

Hosoda ties these problems back into the story by showing various Jinnouchi family members stuck at work

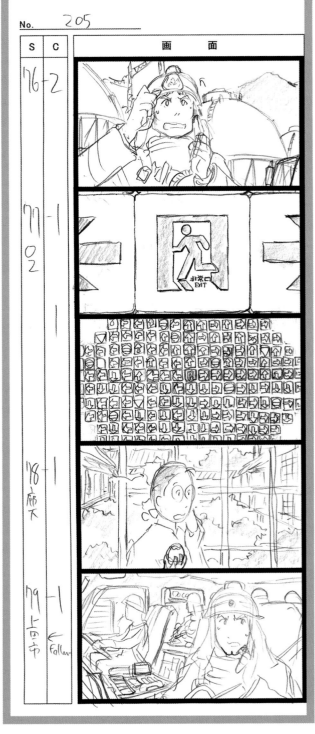

No. 205

Frames from the film (LEFT) and one of Hosoda's storyboards (ABOVE) show Love Machine's actions in OZ causing problems for members of the Jinnouchi family and people all over Japan, tying up traffic and generating false alarm. Hosoda skillfully establishes how actions within the Web affect the real world—and vice versa.

OPPOSITE Storyboards and frames from the film show Love Machine gaining power by absorbing other users' accounts and avatars. The mandala that appears is one manisfestation of his growing power.

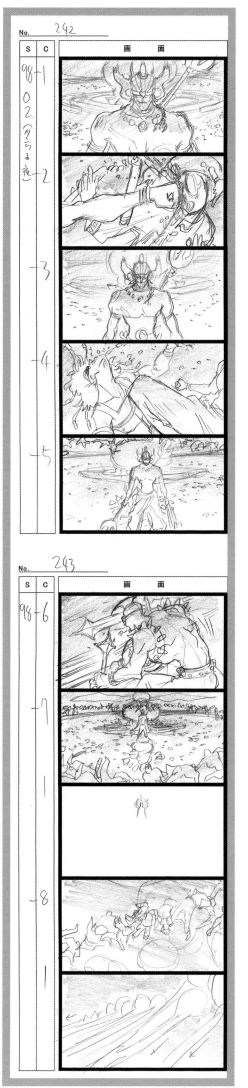

or marooned in traffic, calling to say they'll be late—or may miss the ninetieth birthday celebration altogether. Impatient with her family's dithering about a party when so much more is clearly at stake, Sakae goes into action—using a rotary phone. A woman of considerable social prominence, she galvanizes relatives, neighbors, and politicians into action. She doesn't ask for superhuman efforts, but she coaxes and bullies people into doing whatever they can to alleviate the situation. The message is clear: Community is an extension of family, and everyone must pull together.

As he absorbs more and more users' accounts and avatars—including Kenji's—Love Machine grows in power and menace until he threatens the Earth itself by taking control of a space probe. Crashing it onto a city would cause unparalleled destruction and loss of life. Inspired by Sakae's example, Kenji emerges from his gloomy shell and leads the Jinnouchi clan into battle. Introverted and insecure, Kenji's small, uncertain movements mean he's in constant danger of being eclipsed by Natsuki's louder, more flamboyant relatives.

"A lot of animators are, by nature, on the more introverted side, so they can definitely relate to how Kenji must be feeling and what kind of movements or gestures he might use," says animation director Hiroyuki Aoyama. "But the animation really goes back to the director's storyboards and verbal communication with the animators. A lot of the performances are baked into the storyboard. It served as a central pillar for anyone working on the project."

Artists have usually avoided crowd scenes in handdrawn animated features: The time and effort needed to draw so many characters (referred to in the animation industry as "line mileage") makes these scenes expensive, as well as difficult. But the Jinnouchi clan encompasses four generations, from matrons and senior uncles to young parents with small children, all of them eating, arguing, and running around the ancestral estate.

"In *Summer Wars*, we're looking at a family of twenty-odd members. How many movies have given that many characters identities of their own?" Hosoda muses. "Maybe the *Godfather* films. When that many people from different backgrounds with different characters converge, it lends itself to very interesting filmmaking. All the characters in *Summer Wars* are protagonists! I love when they started 'preparing for war,' moving computer equipment, preparing food. Kenji is moved by the people around him to break his own limits."

In the *Japan Times*, Mark Schilling commented, "Despite the dozens of characters—including the twenty-seven members of Natsuki's extended family—a surprisingly large number emerge as individuals, not just cartoony faces in the crowd."

"The character designs came from Yoshiyuki Sadamoto, who worked on *Evangelion*," adds Aoyama. "My role was to translate his sketches into something that was animatable.

In the scenes where there are a lot of characters, they all had their own individuality. I would give credit to Sadamoto and to Hosoda, who spoke at length about how each character would behave.

"A really good animator, Takayuki Hamada, animated all the scenes where the family is eating in a huge group," he adds. "Matching the right animator to the right scene is a big part of what Hosoda has to think about. My job was made a lot easier by how good the animator assignments were."

The clan initially tries to trap Love Machine in a cyberprison, following the tactics Jinnouchi samurai used in the seventeenth century, but a well-intended second cousin mistakenly allows their supercomputer to overheat, enabling the monster to escape. With the clock ticking down toward a possibly deadly catastrophe, the family launches a final gamble—literally and figuratively.

Exploiting the program's weakness for competitive games, they challenge Love Machine to play the traditional Japanese card game koi-koi, betting the family's avatars. The walls of the OZ Casino suggest an Edo-era gold leaf screen, but with silhouettes of dinosaurs moving across its panels. "I created several drafts of different Japanese-style designs, but could not get the 'OK' from Hosoda," says Jojo. "He finally told me, 'Let's try it with some dinosaurs!' I put together a design he signed off on."

By this time, Love Machine has grown into a gigantic, pointillist monster comprised of countless stolen avatars. Its long rabbit ears were taken from OZ martial arts champion King Kazma, the avatar of Natsuki's sullen cousin Kazuma. The sinister image of Love Machine looming over the girl conveys the power of the menace she's confronting: Natsuki stands alone, like a beacon before a storm.

"Hosoda is really good at setting up this kind of conflict, especially in the storyboarding phase," comments Nishiyama. "He uses longer cuts in the beginning to establish the scope and the grandeur of what the audience is seeing, then transitions to quicker, action cuts. He'll punch in for a close-up, then pull the camera away again, which gives that grand feeling of dynamism. The world of OZ is no exception to the techniques Hosoda employs.

"What separates Hosoda's work is the technical skill in what he does: There's no wasted camera movements," he continues. "Some of that might be attributed to his days at

As the Jinnouchi clan "start preparing for war" against Love Machine, one uncle delivers a massive computer more suitable for the Department of Defense.

Large blocks of ice preserve Sakae's body,
which has been laid out in her house.

Toei, because we were in close proximity to a lot of artists who worked in live-action. I think their ideas rubbed off on Hosoda. You look at animation today and even live-action, and the camera goes everywhere. It goes places it really shouldn't. But with Hosoda's work it's his perspective and the audience's perspective, which is a very clearly defined look into the world of the film."

During the battle, Natsuki emerges as a complex, layered individual. When she challenges Love Machine, she's scared, and for very good reasons. Although she knows her boisterous relatives are supporting her, she yells at them to shut up so she can concentrate on the koi-koi game. The stylized whales John and Yoko ("the guardian angels of OZ") honor her courage, granting her "an auspicious rare item." (An older relative comments, "I have no idea what that means, but thank you.") A blizzard of cherry blossoms transforms Natsuki's costume into the traditional white robe and red divided skirt of a Shinto shrine maiden.

Tomm Moore, the Oscar-nominated director of *Wolf-Walkers*, says, "I felt that *Summer Wars* was Hosoda taking off the gloves: A *Digimon* kind of world, but really going heavy with stuff. If you're being authentic about your world-building, then you have to be authentic about how dark things can go."

Natsuki's skill at koi-koi (which she learned from great-grandmother Sakae) enables her to defeat Love Machine, assisted by Kenji's extraordinary mathematical abilities and Kazuma's mastery of kung fu and computer games. As the battle reaches its climax, a German boy offers Natsuki his avatar, asking her to protect his family. Hordes of others join him, giving Natsuki the resources she needs to conquer Love Machine. In a series of rapid cuts, Hosoda shows people of all ages and nationalities watching the battle and silently cheering Natsuki on. These diverse individuals link together, forming a community to crush a foe too powerful to fight individually.

Moved by their faith in her, Natsuki bursts into tears, then sets her jaw and confronts her foe with new confidence. Hosoda keeps the focus on the very human teenagers, not the impressive special effects. None of the characters can rely on superpowers, which gives their victory an immediacy lacking in many other science-fiction adventures ("There are no superheroes and mecha in real life.").

Although Hosoda had said when he began *Summer Wars* that he wanted to depict a Japanese family rather than make a summer blockbuster, the film did become a smash hit. The Blu-ray release broke the previous record set by Hideaki Anno's *Evangelion: 1.0 You Are (Not) Alone*. Hosoda again won the Japanese Academy Award for Best Animation Film, as well as the Tokyo Anime Awards for Animation of the Year, Art Direction, Character Design, Director, Original Story and Screenplay. *Summer Wars* was named Best Animated Feature Film at the Sitges Festival in Spain, and received an award for new media from the Japanese Ministry of Economy, Trade, and Industry at the annual Digital Content Association of Japan convention.

NATSUKI PLAYS KOI-KOI

Koi-Koi is a Japanese game played with the *Hanafuda* cards that were developed during the early nineteenth century. The images on the cards represent the months of the year and flowers, animals and phases of the moon associated with them. (Nintendo was founded in 1889 to produce and market handmade *Hanafuda* cards.) The members of the Jinnouchi clan are enthusiastic players, and Natsuki learned the game from her great-grandmother.

BELOW Hosoda's storyboard indicates how the camera would pan down Natsuki's avatar as she prepares to challenge Love Machine.

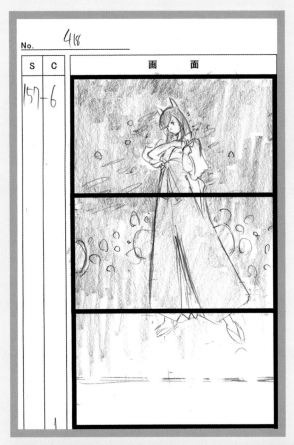

LEFT The background suggests an Edo-era gilded screen—populated with the silhouettes of dinosaurs. An anonymous German user offers Natsuki his account (BOTTOM), asking her to protect his family.

ABOVE The two animation drawings and the frames from the film show Natsuki's determination as she battles Love Machine.

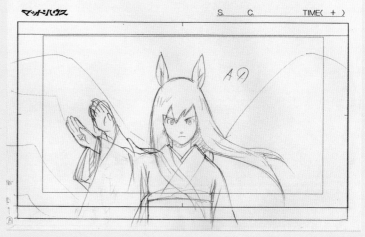

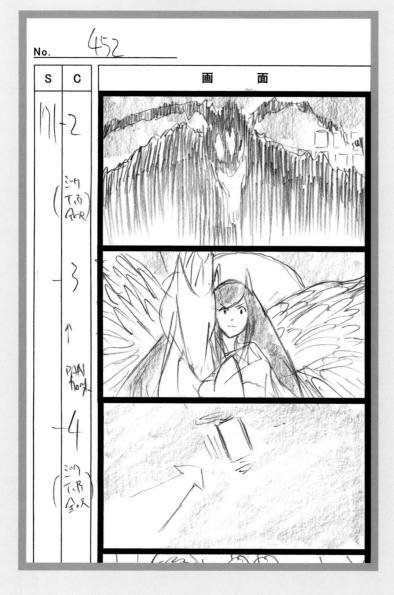

No. 452

S	C	画　面

The battle continues:

TOP Two layout drawings indicating Natsuki's movements

ABOVE A frame from the film and two animation drawings.
The notes and simple diagrams on the drawings are
instructions for the animators.

LEFT Another panel from Hosoda's storyboard

FOLLOWING SPREAD A dramatic image showcases Natsuki's
bravery as she faces her foe, a pointillist monster bloated
with countless stolen accounts.

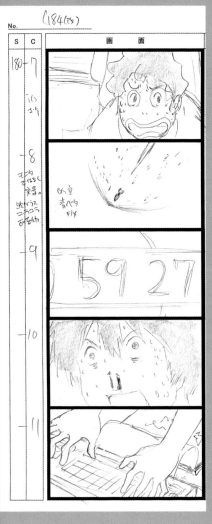

No. 484(改)

S	C	画面
180	-7	
	-8	
	-9	
	-10	
	-11	

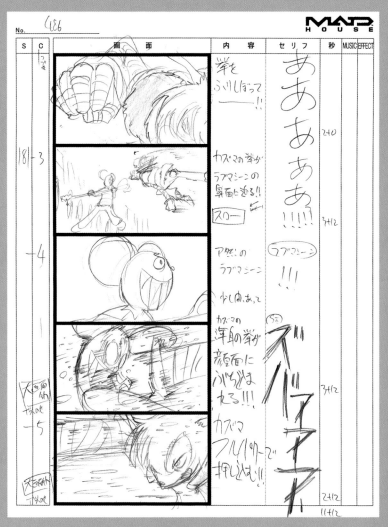

No. 486　MAD HOUSE

S	C	画面	内容	セリフ	秒	MUSIC EFFECT
			拳を ふりしぼって ――!!	ああ ああ ああ !!!!	2+0	
181	-3		カズマの拳が ラブマシーンの 鼻面に迫る!! スロー		3+12	
	-4		ア然の ラブマシーン	ラブマシーン !!!		
			少しぬ、あって カズマの渾身の拳が 鼻っ面にバチッと える!!!	スバッ	3+12	
	-5		カズマ フルパワーで 押しこむ!!	ヴァイン	2+12	
					11+12	

No. 485

S	C	画面
180	-12	NAVISTAR14　NAVISTAR15　NAVISTAR16
181	-1	
02		
	-1	
	-1	
	-2	
	-13	

No. 487

S	C	画面	内容	セリフ	秒	MUSIC EFFECT
181	-6		181-4Fからポ ひしげていく鼻面!!!		2+12	
	-7		181-5Fからポ カズマ ねじ込ませ!!			
	-8		181-4Fから ひしげて いく ラブマシーン!!!		2+12	
	-9		一瞬で全身が ポリゴンになった今田 する!!		5+0	
182	-1		180-12同ポ [発信ほまみ] の文字出る。 (英語表記)	フォン!	3+12	
					1+0	
					14+12	

00:59:94

Enter repair code:

NAVSATT5ann　NAVSATT6ann　NAVSATT7ann

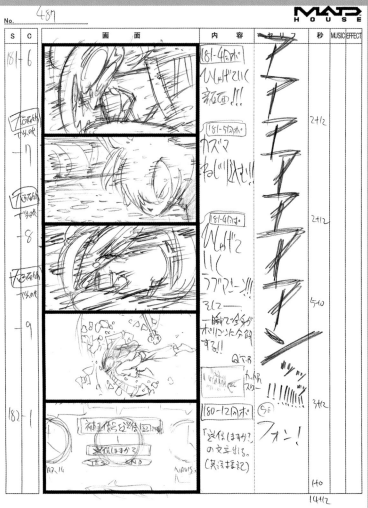

LEFT AND OPPOSITE **Natsuki** has reduced Love Machine to two accounts. Kenji uses his extraordinary mathematical abilities and Kazuma uses his martial arts skills as King Kazma to deliver the coup de grâce before Love Machine can re-infect the security system of OZ. Unlike American studios, where crews of artists work on the storyboards, Hosoda and other Japanese directors board the entire film themselves.

BELOW **Hosoda draws King Kazma for a fan.**

The film earned rave reviews in Japan, the United States, and in Europe, where it screened at the Annecy International Animation Festival and the Berlin and Locarno International Film Festivals. In the *Japan Times*, Schilling wrote, "Hosoda and his team, including animation director Hiroyuki Aoyama, action animation director Tatsuzo Nishita, and character designer Yoshiyuki Sadamoto, have produced scenes of animated spectacle that, in their dazzling fluency of motion and untethered brilliance of invention, makes the usual SF/fantasy anime look childish and dull."

In *Première*, Gérard Delorme said, "The results are astonishing: The film has a virtuosity worthy of Altman, an ambition equal to Cameron in terms of the interaction of the virtual and the real, and a human complexity akin to Sautet." Justin Sevakis of Anime News Network declared, "Decades from now, *Summer Wars* will be seen as the official arrival of Mamoru Hosoda into the realm of historically important anime directors. It's a near-perfect blend of social satire and science fiction, at once timely and timeless, sardonic and optimistic."

When asked about the international appeal of *Summer Wars*, Hosoda replied, "I attended the US premiere at the New York International Children's Film Festival and was happy to see American audiences enjoying the film. Of course, I want my film to be enjoyed in other countries, but I believe only good local movies can be good international movies."

OPPOSITE Hosoda's storyboards show how the Jinnouchi ancestral compound will be revealed.

ABOVE A layout drawing of the scene; the red rectangles near the center of the image indicate the placement and movement of the camera.

RIGHT A background painting of an interior detail

FOLLOWING SPREAD The background painting evokes the landscape of the Nagano Prefecture in central Honshu.

BACKGROUND DESIGNS

Hosoda wanted the backgrounds to capture the look of Nagano, the home prefecture of his wife's family.

BELOW Two layout drawings looking over the roof of the Jinnouchi house

SECOND FROM BOTTOM Two background paintings in progress, showing the scene at different times of day

BOTTOM The completed paintings: The satellite dishes on the traditional tiled roofs reflect the meeting of modern and ancestral Japan.

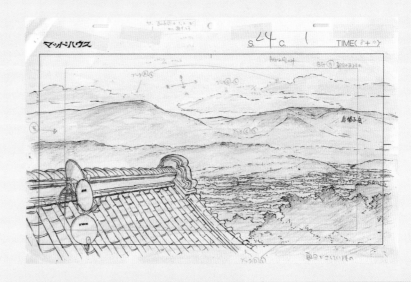

A background painting of enormous cumulus clouds, seen through
a window in the Jinnouchi house, suggests the oppressive heat and
humidity of the Japanese summer.

OZ

The bright colors and rounded shapes of OZ were designed to make the world feel safe and welcoming to all users.

OPPOSITE The graffiti defacing OZ is a visible manifestation of Love Machine's disruptions, which threaten to reduce Japan to chaos. Disney production designer Paul Felix comments, "When Love Machine's attacks occur, OZ's palette makes it seem even more sinister."

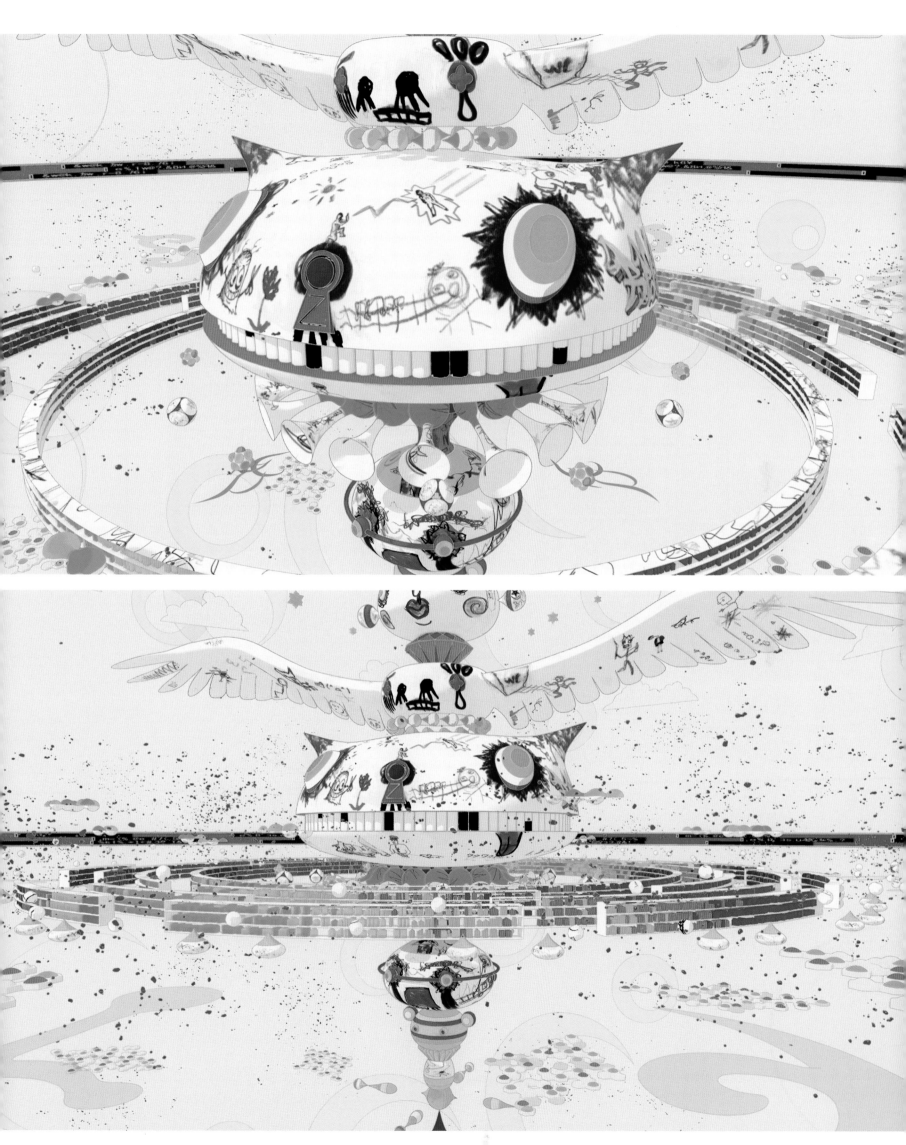

KING KAZMA

When Natsuki's sullen cousin Kazuma Ikezawa was bullied at school, he began studying kung fu with his uncle Mansuke. Kazuma funneled his martial arts and video gaming skills into his avatar, King Kazma. During the title sequence of *Summer Wars,* Kazma defeats a series of challengers in record-breaking time.

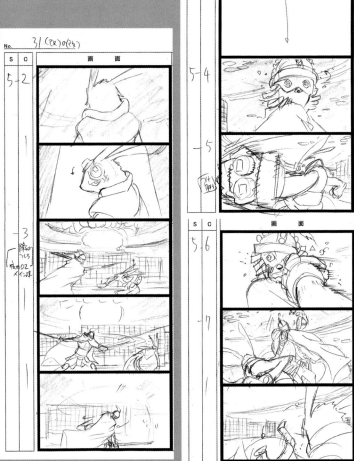

ABOVE Panels from Hosoda's storyboards of the opening fights

BELOW A layout drawing from the scene indicates how the character and the camera will move.

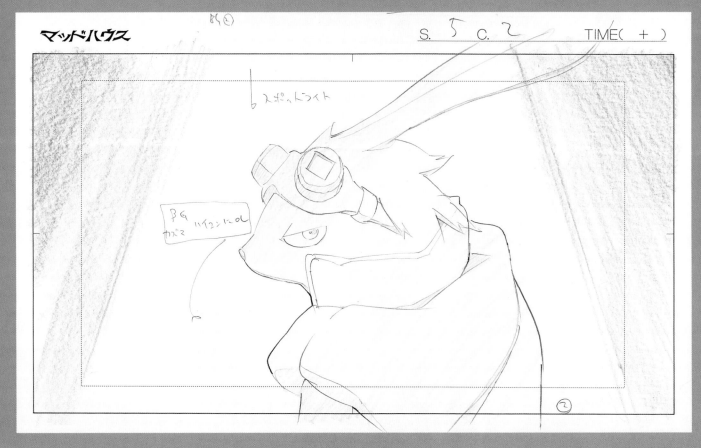

THIS PAGE King Kazma takes on (and takes down) a challenger whose avatar suggests a medieval knight.

FOLLOWING SPREAD King Kazma's roundhouse kick reflects Kazuma's knowledge of martial arts moves.

KING KAZMA ANIMATION SKETCHES

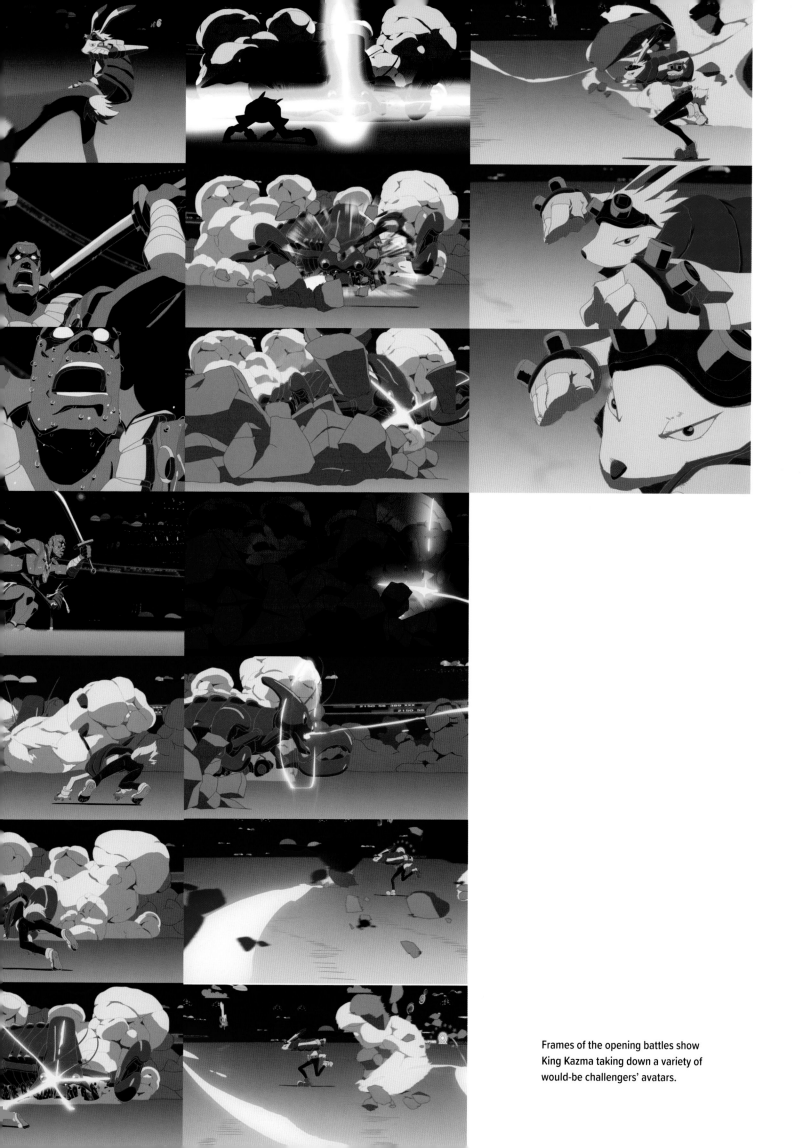

Frames of the opening battles show
King Kazma taking down a variety of
would-be challengers' avatars.

LOVE MACHINE ANIMATION SKETCHES

As the battle with King Kazma begins, Love Machine strikes a preparatory pose and hurls himself at his foe. The sketchy drawings reveal the animator's mind at work.

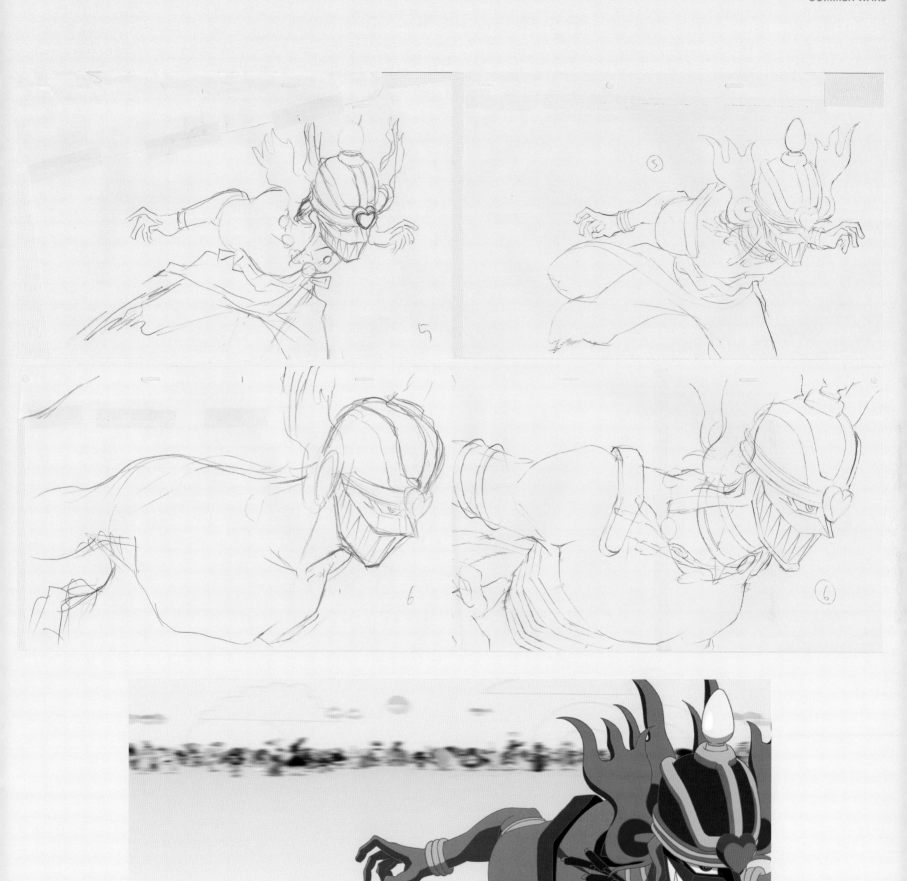

The battle continues between Love Machine and King Kazma. The rougher drawings on the left show the artist creating the complex leaps, kicks, and turns in the martial arts duel. The cleanup drawings on the right feature added details and more polished line work.

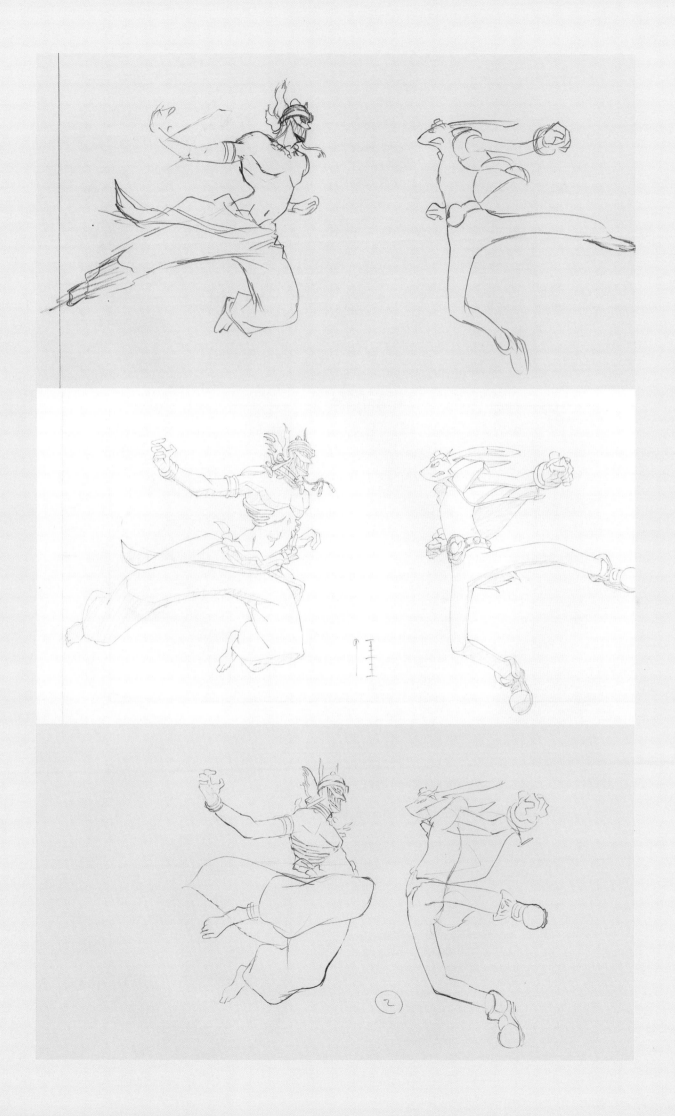

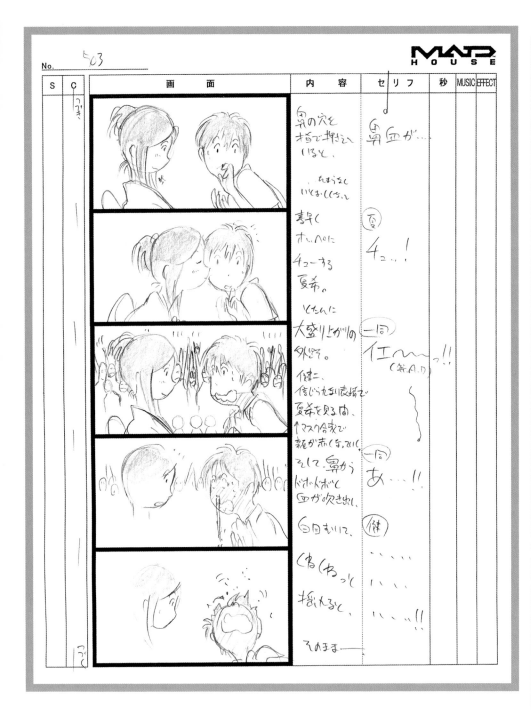

Hosoda's storyboards and frames from the film show Natsuki acting on her growing affection for Kenji.

OPPOSITE The changed expression on Sakae's memorial portrait suggests she approves of Kenji as a partner for Natsuki—and is amused by his overreaction.

MARKETING

Summer Wars–related merchandise included magnets, mugs, plates, and pouches.

OPPOSITE **The poster for** Summer Wars

TENTH ANNIVERSARY

OPPOSITE The poster for the tenth anniversary of the film featured striking new artwork of the cast's avatars.

New merchandise included highly articulated figures of Love Machine and King Kazma, plus water bottles, bags, and T-shirts.

IV. WOLF CHILDREN

Summer Wars became a smash hit. When Hosoda and I talked about what kind of movie we should make next, I said I don't know whether it will be a massive hit or not. And frankly, I don't think that's relevant. You should make what you want. Hosoda said, "The next movie should be in honor of my mother; it should celebrate her life." That was how *Wolf Children* started.

—YUICHIRO SAITO

Wolf Children marked a turning point in director Mamoru

Hosoda's and producer Yuichiro Saito's careers: Producing it led to the founding of Studio Chizu. *Summer Wars* had been partially inspired by Hosoda's introduction into his wife's large family; *Wolf Children* came from an even more personal place.

"Back in 2002, when *Howl's Moving Castle* wasn't going well, Hosoda's mom's health took a turn for the worse, beginning a long battle against illness," Saito explains. "Hosoda took a leave of absence from the animation industry and went home to Toyama to care for her. But an uncle of his, who was a model for one of the characters in *Summer Wars*, told him, 'We'll take care of your mother: You need to pursue your dream. Keep going.' Hosoda says he was 'dragged by the scruff of his neck' back to Tokyo, where he resumed his work as a director. The part-time jobs he took under pseudonyms while he was at Toei paid for his mother's hospital bills. She passed away two months before he finished *Summer Wars*—his first foray into making a big family film. After its completion, he began to put together *Wolf Children* as an homage to his mother. Saito adds, "Hosoda wanted to offer a tribute to his mother's life, one that would express his gratitude for all she had done for him, so he needed a very pure place to work."

The need for a "pure place to work" came at a bad time. Saito continues, "Madhouse was going through financial troubles. My mentor in the industry, Masao Maruyama [the co-founder of Madhouse], called me one night. He was in a hospital. I thought, *This is the end; he's going to say his last words to me and give me his will*. Instead, I found him rather healthy and in good spirits, drinking a Coca-Cola. He said, 'Saito, it's time for you to evaluate where you are and what to do next. I singled you out because I think you need to think hard and act on it.' "

Hosoda adds, "At Madhouse we produced *The Girl Who Leapt Through Time* and *Summer Wars*. I thought, *This is great! We're on this amazing track, and I get to keep making movies*. But with Madhouse experiencing financial problems, I talked to Saito a lot: 'What am I going to do? We're not going to be able to make movies!' We hoped that Studio Chizu ["map" in Japanese] would be a treasure map that would guide us to where we needed to go."

Smaller studios, often built around a single artist or group of artists, play an important role in Japanese animation. But Studio Chizu was initially created for a single purpose: to make *Wolf Children*. None of the principals expected it to become an ongoing concern.

"We created the studio to produce Hosoda's next film," states co-executive producer Nozomu Takahashi of Nippon TV. "Unlike Studio Khara with Hideaki Anno's *Evangelion*,

OPPOSITE **Ame and Yuki's self-portraits as humans and wolves. Artist: Chie Morimoto**

Studio Chizu didn't have a strong intellectual property around which we could build an organization. It was much closer to the original Studio Ghibli model. We formed the studio to produce the film and tried to bring on partners or backers, as Tokuma Shoten had helped back Studio Ghibli. Nippon TV helped produce *Summer Wars*; there was a strong relationship there, and Kadokawa was linked to *The Girl Who Leapt Through Time*. It was very important to bring these two allies into the fold at Studio Chizu's inception."

Although he conceived the story for the new film alone, Hosoda wrote the screenplay with Satoko Okudera, who had worked with him on *The Girl Who Leapt Through Time* and *Summer Wars*. Hosoda had enjoyed their previous collaborations, but it felt odd to have another writer make changes to a tribute to his mother. Still, Hosoda praises Okudera as "a valuable asset to the Japanese movie industry. There aren't many people who can do what she can."

Hana, a diligent nineteen-year-old student, notices a quiet, lanky young man in her history class taking notes, but he doesn't have the textbook. She offers to lend him hers. As they spend time together, the cheerful girl and reclusive boy fall in love. He reluctantly reveals he is a wolfman: not a Western-style werewolf, but the kind of shapeshifter that often appears in Japanese folktales. He can change form at will, and he is the last of his line: Wolves were exterminated in Japan at the beginning of the twentieth century.

In contrast to the boisterous arguments in *Summer Wars*, the romance between Hana and the Wolfman develops largely in silence, accompanied by Masakatsu Takagi's delicate score. "Would Hana and the Wolfman use words in their romance and courtship? Probably not," says Hosoda thoughtfully. "The Wolfman's breed must live mostly in silence and keep their secrets very close to their hearts. Their attraction is different; they wouldn't use words to get to know each other. Simultaneously, I wanted to depict Hana's capacity to understand those very few words.

"If this were a romantic comedy, there would be a lot of exchanges of words and jabs as their relationship built," he adds. "But we're looking at a creature who's on the verge of extinction, who has a history and a very deep personal story. Hana must be able to grasp all of that, come to an understanding, and find romance there. Words wouldn't play a large role in their relationship."

RIGHT Hosoda's storyboards from the film. This sequence neither has nor needs dialogue to communicate its emotional power.

OPPOSITE The Wolfman reveals his true nature to Hana, in these sensitive animation drawings.

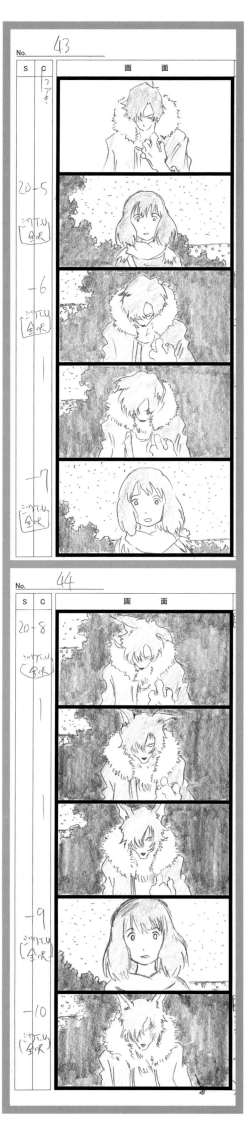

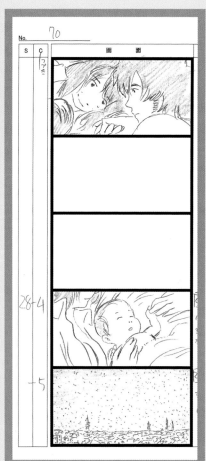

Instead of the happy wedding that Disney's Cinderella and Ariel enjoy, Hana and the Wolfman's relationship leads to a baby girl, Yuki ("Snow"), and a boy, Ame ("Rain"). The Wolfman delivers them, fearing they might assume puppy form. He becomes a gently loving husband and father, and Hana is shattered when he's killed trying to provide for his family.

"The first time I encountered Hosoda was around Christmas of 2011: I received a poster for *Wolf Children* and an invitation to participate in its production," says Takagi. "There was no screenplay, no storyboard. But having seen *The Girl Who Leapt Through Time* and *Summer Wars*, I knew I wanted to work on it. Our next interaction was when I received the screenplay; it was a really compelling story. We met, discussed music and composition. I only had about three months to complete the score. Hosoda gave me the screenplay and a storyboard and said, 'Make it however you like. All the information I need to convey is in the storyboard.'"

Since the children have inherited their father's shape-shifting ability, raising them in a tiny Tokyo apartment proves impossible. The neighbors complain about the crying and barking; nosy officials try to check up on the children. In a darkly comic moment, Hana calls both a pediatrician and a veterinarian for advice when Yuki accidentally eats a silica packet.

The search for the freedom her children need leads Hana to the northern mountains, where the Wolfman grew up. In much of rural Japan, villages are being abandoned as the population ages and young people move to cities. Hana finds a ramshackle house with only a few hardy farmers for neighbors. The real estate agent can't believe she actually wants such an isolated house. But the rent is very cheap, and Hosoda makes it clear that Hana must live on a very limited budget.

OPPOSITE **The birth of their daughter, Yuki, strengthens the bond between Hana and the Wolfman. Hosoda's storyboards, frames from the film, and a touching animation drawing.**

RIGHT **Three lively drawings show Yuki effortlessly transitioning from human child to wolf pup while her brother, Ame, looks on.**

Life in a tiny Tokyo apartment with two energetic children/puppies proves impossible.

OPPOSITE, TOP Animation drawings of Yuki

OPPOSITE, BOTTOM A drawing overlaying a background of the apartment

RIGHT Frames from the scene

ABOVE Hosoda's storyboards show Hana trying to cope with her active children.

Costume supervisor Daisuke Iga explains, "If you change a color in animation, you can make an infinite number of new costumes—but we intentionally didn't do that for Hana. We only gave her five pairs of pants, and she wears the same coat she had as a student. We took a similar approach to what I would do on a live-action film by intentionally recycling the same costumes.

"When I read the screenplay, I got the sense Hosoda was really going for a realistic approach. I think he wanted me to bring a perspective from the live-action world," he adds. "In one scene, Yuki wears a one-piece with a snow-flake pattern stitched by her mother. I wanted to see if this type of stitching could actually be done, so I made a sample to ensure we brought that dose of reality to the animation."

Hana is painfully aware of her limited resources as she tries to adjust to rural life. She has to repair the house's leaky roof and clean away years of accumulated dust and grime. She knows nothing about growing vegetables and her first crops wither. But her perseverance, good manners, and kind heart gradually win the respect and affection of her skeptical neighbors. As he did in *Summer Wars*, Hosoda shows the importance of community: The small group of farm families share produce, equipment, and knowledge. Their acceptance of Hana and her family contrasts with the isolation she endured in Tokyo.

The old-fashioned farmhouse, with its sliding panels, aged tatami mats, and large garden, becomes almost a character in the story, as do the Jinnouchi ancestral compound in *Summer Wars*, Kumatetsu's messy bachelor's quarters in *The Boy and the Beast*, and Kun's Western-style home in *Mirai*.

"In animation, when you're trying to depict people, there are two very important aspects that have far more weight than they would in a live-action movie: 'What do these people eat?' And 'Where do these people live?'" explains Hosoda. "In a live-action production, you don't have to pay as much attention to these details. You're dealing with actors and real-life people, so it's easier to imagine how they live. In animation, it's all just a series of illustrations. To make the characters feel alive, we have to create that sense of reality. We can't just assume that people will feel and understand.

"I accidentally found a house that looked like one Hana would choose to live in, when we were driving in the countryside, location scouting" he adds with a chuckle. "I walked up to the people and said, 'Can you please let us go through your house and take photos?' Creating the environment in which the protagonist's journey unfolds gives it that extra layer."

Costume supervisor Daisuke Iga (LEFT) made the clothes for the characters. The finished garments enabled the animators to see how the fabric moved and draped to create more believable animation. Iga notes, "With live action, a lot of the costume restrictions are defined by the actors' anatomy, including their height and size; for women, there are a lot of proportions you have to consider. In animation, there's a little more flexibility."

45 - 3

Hosoda's insistence that the environments reflect the characters' personalities carried over to the other artists. Takagi says thoughtfully, "Going through the screenplay and storyboards, it occurred to me that motherhood is the overarching theme throughout the movie: a mother figure watching over everyone. The old house protects the family, so you give the house its own sounds. And there's the actual mother, who sings lullabies to the kids. Thinking about the different maternal figures and their dialogue is where I drew a lot of my inspiration."

Even in the countryside, keeping the children's supernatural abilities secret remains difficult. The neighbors wonder about the odd "dogs" they sometimes see when they drop by, and they're puzzled that the wild pigs that have ravaged everyone else's gardens don't bother Hana's. (The scent of wolf urine scares them off.)

But life in the country offers a freedom Hana and her children could never find in Tokyo. Excited by the beauty of the first snowfall, Hana runs through the forest with Ame and Yuki in their wolf forms. Takagi's upbeat, Prokofiev-inflected melodies lend energy to the exhilarating sequence. For the first time, Ame attempts to hunt, attacking a kingfisher. Although he nearly drowns in an icy stream, the experience marks a turning point in his development.

As young people leave rural Japan for the cities, houses—and entire villages—are being abandoned. Hana is able to get an old farmhouse very cheaply.

ABOVE A background of the neglected house

FOLLOWING SPREAD A computer-rendered image of the interior, with its old beams, sliding panels, and tatami mats

PAGES 116–117 A background painting of the same interior shows the soot on the beams, the wear on the panels, and the dust on the mats.

PAGE 118 Hosoda's storyboards indicate how the camera would move through the scene, introducing the viewer to Hana's new home.

PAGE 119 Additional storyboards show Hana working to turn the derelict farmhouse into a comfortable home for her children.

S	C	画　面	内　容	セリフ	秒	MUSIC	EFFECT
45-4			しかしよく見ると土壁がところどころ崩れていたり、窓が抜けてビニールが貼られていたり。	修繕費、バカにならないよ〜〜。	2+12		
-5			縁側の窓。ガラスが抜けてガムテープで乱暴に補修してあったり。	空き家っフーより……	2+0		
-6			暗い土間に佇む花。声のする方を見る。	あ、土足でいいですよ。	(2+12)		
			開きづらい扉を懸命に開けている黒田からT.B.　朽ちた大広間。畳が剥くられ、床板が腐ってる。巨大な梁が交差する吹き抜け。		G-0		
-7				ほとんど廃屋だものこれ。〈ドア開43 A.D〉でも一応〜			

1340

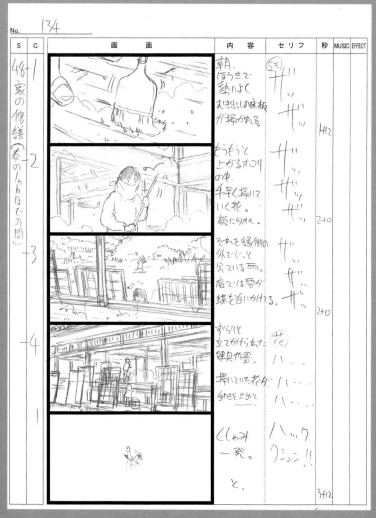

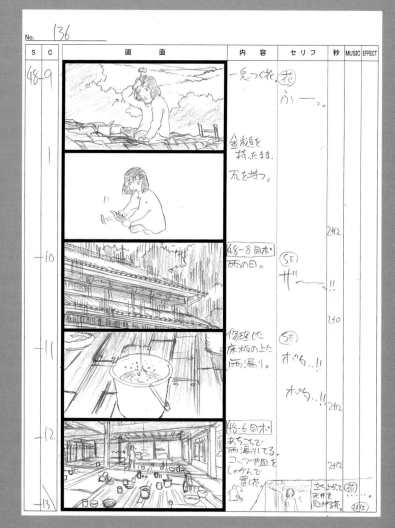

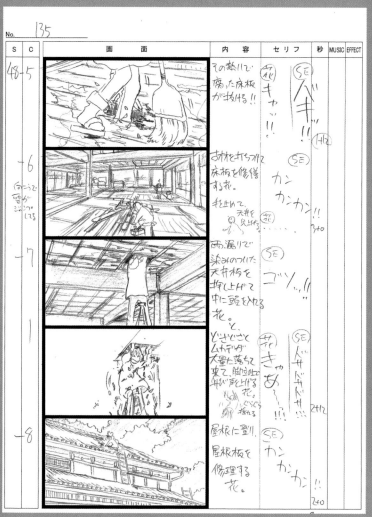

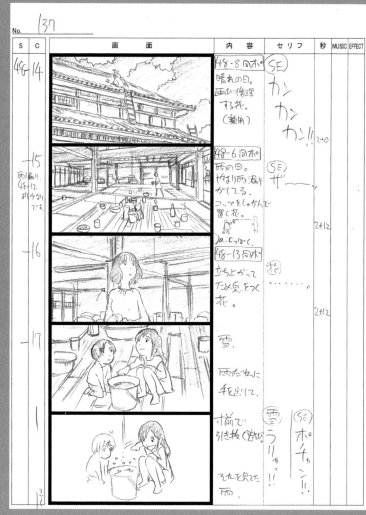

No. 134

S・C	内容	セリフ	秒	MUSIC	EFFECT
48-1 家の修繕 （春の1ヶ月ほどの間）	朝。ほうきで勢いよくむき出しの床板が掃かれる。	(SE)ザッ!!	4+12		
-2	もうもうと上がるホコリの中。手早く掃いていく花。額に夕れ。	ザッ ザッ ザッ	2+0		
-3	それを縁側の外でじっと見ている雨。庭では雪が蝶を追いかける。	ザッ ザッ ザッ	2+0		
-4	ずらりと立てかけられた建具や畳。掃いていた花が動きを止めて	(花)ハ…… ハ…… ハ……			
	くしゃみ一発。と。	ハックッション!!	3+12		

No. 135

S・C	内容	セリフ	秒	MUSIC	EFFECT
48-5	その勢いで腐った床板が抜ける!!	(花)キャッ!! (SE)ベキッ!!	1+12		
-6 向こうで雪が遊んでる	古材を打ちつけて床板を修繕する花。手を止めて天井を見上げる花。	(SE)カンカンカン!! (花)	2+0		
-7	雨漏りで染みのついた天井板を押し上げて中に頭を入れる花。と。	(SE)ゴツ…!!			
	どさどさとムカデが天井から落ちて来て脳裏の中で声を上げる花。	(花)きゃあ (SE)バサバサバサ!!	2+12		
-8	屋根に登り屋根板を修理する花。	(SE)カンカン!!	2+0		

No. 136

S・C	内容	セリフ	秒	MUSIC	EFFECT
48-9	金槌を持ったまま、瓦を持つ。	一見つけた(花)ふー。			
-10	48-8同木 雨の日。	(SE)ザー…!!	2+12		
-11	修理した床板の上に雨漏り。	(SE)ポチャ…!! ポチャ…!!	2+0		
-12	48-6同木 あちこちで雨漏りしてる。コップや皿をしゃがんで置く花。		2+12		
-13	立ち上がって天井を見上げる花。(花)		2+12		

No. 137

S・C	内容	セリフ	秒	MUSIC	EFFECT
48-14	48-8同木 晴れの日。瓦を修理する花。（薬用）	(SE)カンカン!!	2+0		
-15 雨漏り、48-12より少しへってる	48-6同木 雨の日。やはり雨漏りがしてる。コップをしゃがんで置く花。手をつかなくて。	(SE)ザー…!!	2+12		
-16	48-13同木 立ち上がってため息をつく花。	(花)……	2+12		
-17	雪。雨だまりに手を出して。手前で引き抜き（返す）。それを見てた雨。	(雪)ラリラ (SE)ポチャ…!!			

Yuki desperately wants to go to school and live only as a human, although she's dismayed to learn that the girls in her class don't share her interest in snakes, bugs, and small animals bones. A rare burst of anger that causes her to partially transform establishes a bond with her classmate Sohei, who is clearly taken with her. Ame, in contrast, skips school and explores the mountains as a wolf. He's upset by picture books that depict wolves as villains. His lessons come not from textbooks, but a wise, aged fox. The children's diverging paths become clear when a typhoon strikes: Yuki stays at school with Sohei, waiting for her mother; Ame plunges into the forest to look after his mentor.

"When I'm editing, I really immerse myself in what the characters are feeling; I become part of the story," says Shigeru Nishiyama, who has edited all of Hosoda's personal films. "During the menacing storm, I was feeling what the characters were feeling while cutting it together. During the typhoon, Ame emerges as the son of a wolf. The timing and the gaps in the dialogue really changed a lot from the very first edit to the final cut. Hosoda and I spent a lot of time developing that scene."

Hana learns to accept her children's choices and encourages them to find paths that feel right to them. She wonders how their father would react, casting wistful glances at his driver's license photograph on the family Buddhist altar. Although she cautions them to keep their shapeshifting abilities secret, she never tries to force Ame and Yuki to be other than who and what they are. Hana makes sacrifices for her family, but she does so willingly. She remains quiet, gentle, and warmly maternal. Animation is an art of caricature that exaggerates movements and expressions: Hana's small, modest motions required delicate, focused work from the animators.

"As a rule, Japanese people don't use a lot of big gestures that lend themselves to exaggerated acting," says key animator Hiroyuki Aoyama. "The expressions are very important, and it all comes back to the storyboards, which serve as a blueprint for everyone. The storyboards, combined with Hosoda's explanations, influence how characters are animated on the screen."

Ame explores the animal side of his nature.

TOP An animation drawing of Ame capturing his first prey

ABOVE The scene in the finished film

RIGHT Editor Shigeru Nishiyama, who has worked on all of Hosoda's personal features, comments, "When we're timing things out and editing it, we are very mindful of dialogue. Because *Wolf Children* is a more intimate drama, we approached it a lot more delicately than we would sequences that featured a lot more action."

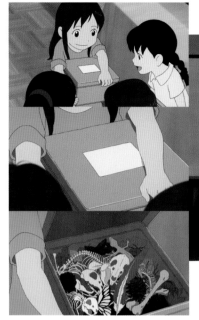

In contrast to her brother, Ame, Yuki wants to live only as a human.

ABOVE An animation drawing of Yuki opening her box of personal treasures—which frighten the other girls in her class

At school, Sohei upsets Yuki to the point where she begins to transform and strikes him, injuring his ear. Yet the two bond.

LEFT Hosoda's storyboard shows the camera move in the scene.

BELOW Two frames of the dramatic moment

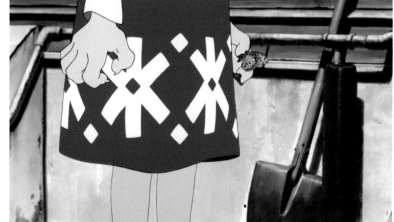

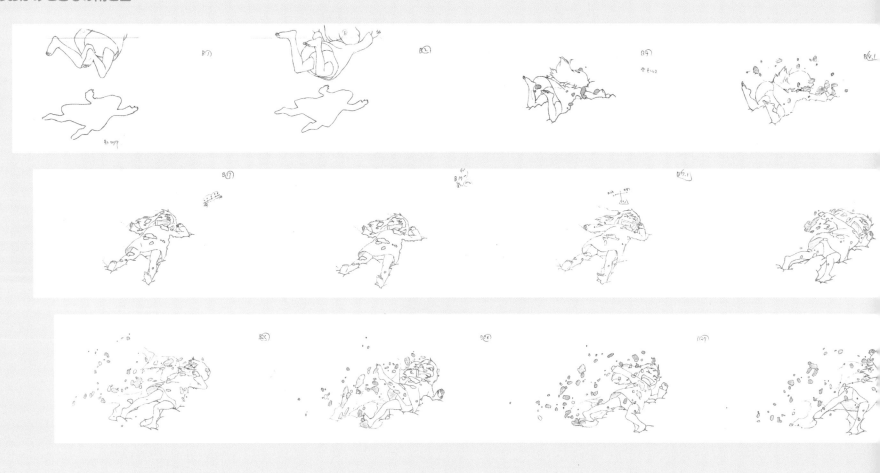

"It came down to Hosoda's love for that character; my job was to take that love and ensure it was reflected in the animation," adds animation director Takaaki Yamashita. "Taking Hosoda's intentions and expressing them doesn't leave much room for interpretation. It's all about translating what Hosoda's looking for onto the screen."

Ame and Yuki age several years during the course of the film and appear in both human and wolf form, as does their father. Creating a character who is recognizable in different bodies and at different ages also posed challenges for the animators. The characters' appearances and movements must suggest consistency and change simultaneously. But Hosoda feels the shifting forms of the main characters are essential part of his story.

"The changes in form aren't too far from what we do as humans: Around some people, you maintain a facade or a mask; with others you can be your true self. Humans are two, three layers deep," he explains. "The visual transformations of these characters represent a similar idea. The Wolfman has to be human when he is part of human society, but in front of those with whom he feels truly vulnerable can he show his wolf side.

"With Ame and Yuki, there are obvious shifts that occur as they move from childhood toward adulthood," Hosoda continues. "Yuki is a very active child. As she grows and adapts to society, a lot of that energy is suppressed by the social constructs around her. Ame grows up a very fearful child, but meeting his mentor figure awakens his more bestial, feral side—he grows in that regard. It's not just the wolf/human transformation: There's the duality of childhood and adulthood. This duality plus time creates a very interesting dynamic. I'm really showing the many different faces of a single human in these characters."

Wolf Children was well received by the world animation community, and when Tomm Moore, the Oscar-nominated director of *The Secret of Kells*, began a film based on Irish legends about shapeshifting human-wolves, he took another look.

"At the very beginning of *WolfWalkers,* I watched *Wolf Children* just to make sure we weren't going in the exact same direction," Moore recalls. "There's some overlap with themes we deal with in *WolfWalkers*, but Hosoda goes much more realistic than we would dare. It's tricky what he pulls off, because it's almost a single line around a pretty academic rendering of a wolf. And he has these transformation sequences which are so charmingly done where the kids shake like a dog, then they're wolves."

Yuki experiences her first snowfall in the country.

ABOVE AND OPPOSITE, TOP **She rolls gleefully in the snow in these vivid animation drawings.** OPPOSITE, BOTTOM LEFT **Hosoda's storyboard of her leap into the snow.** OPPOSITE, MIDDLE AND BOTTOM RIGHT **Two images from the film.**

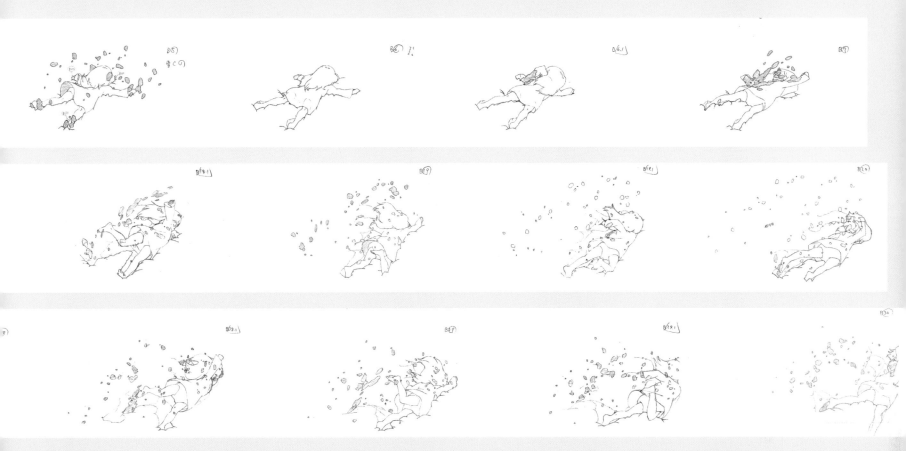

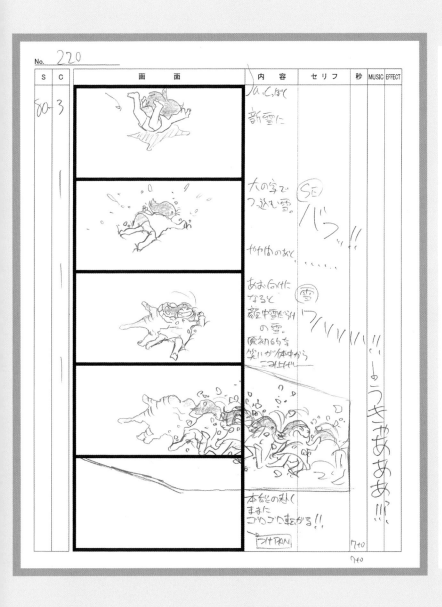

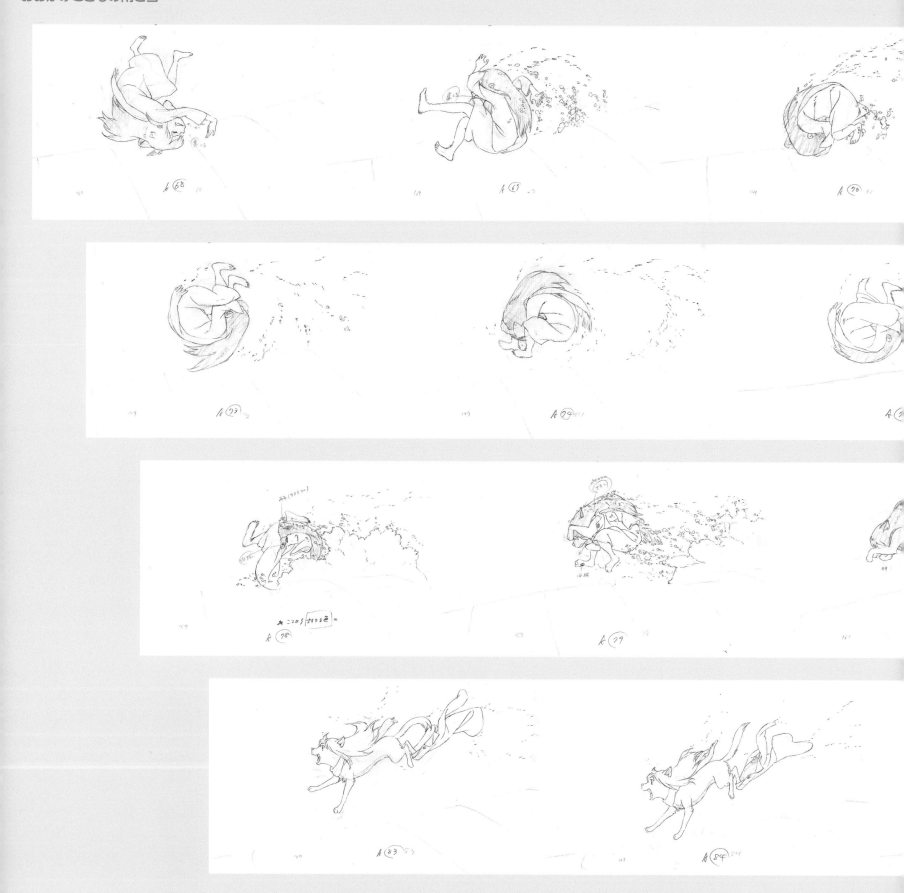

Yuki dives and somersaults down a slope, assuming her wolf
form and shedding her nightie as she goes, in these lively
animation drawings.

OPPOSITE, BOTTOM **Three frames from the sequence**

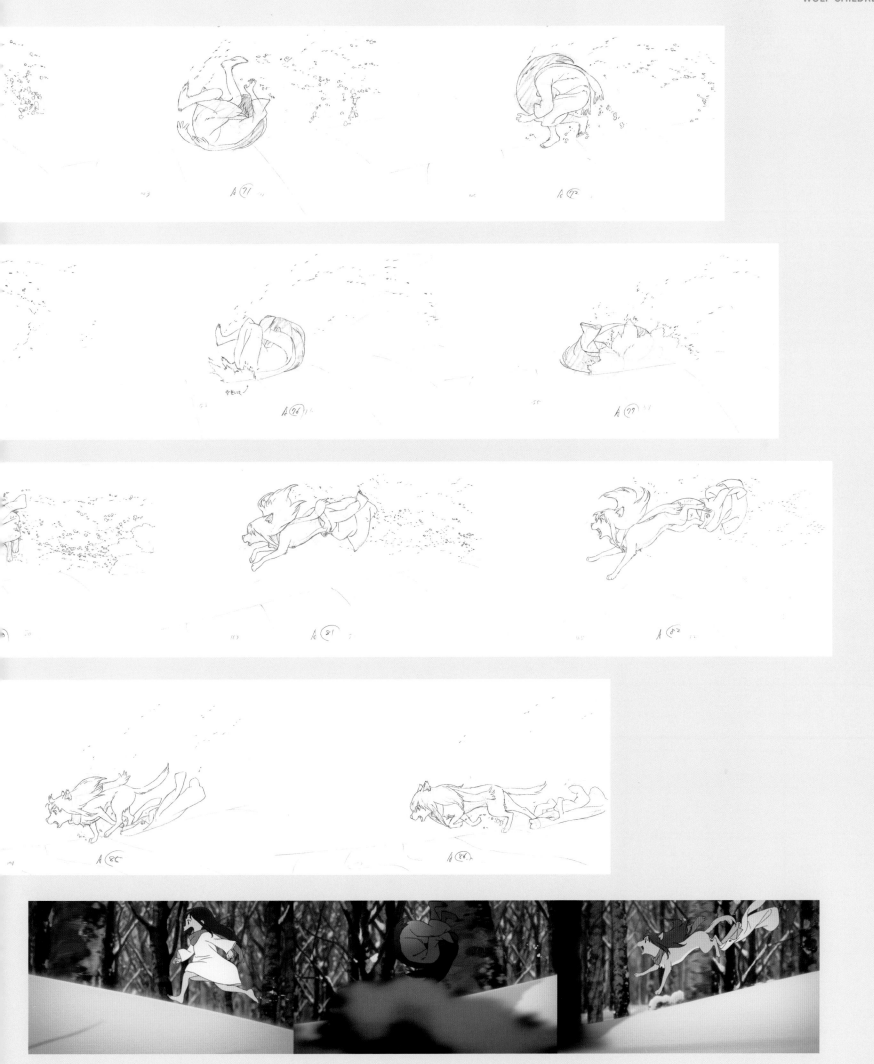

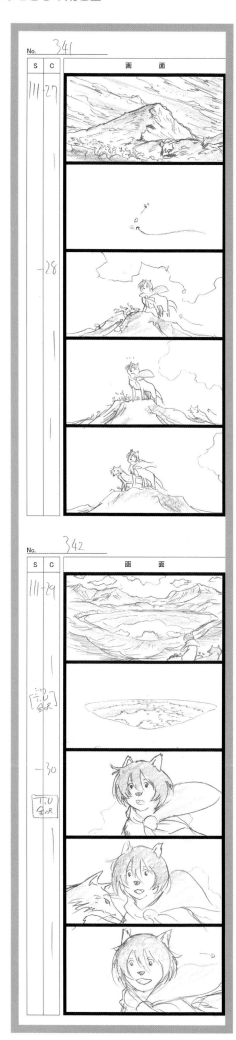

LEFT Hosoda's storyboards show Ame learning about the forest as a wolf under the tutelage of a wise, old fox.

ABOVE Frames from the sequence

Moore also feels a bond with the combination of fantasy and reality Hosoda brings to the worlds in his films. "Even if we're drawing really stylized environments, it's always based on research and putting in details people will recognize," Moore adds. "Every element in a house we design is carefully based on research, even if we're drawing it in a stylized way, and that's what Hosoda does as well. Everything in his films has a suchness that it's from lived experience. There's a sense the objects have

been used over and over again; they're not one-off cartoon props."

Both Irish and Japanese folktales describe cordial relations between humans and wolves. As they researched *WolfWalkers*, Moore and his artists discovered stories about wolves protecting people who treated them with kindness and respect. Oliver Cromwell began exterminating the wolves when he came to Ireland in 1649. Hosoda counters that in Japan prior to the Meiji era (1868–1912), there was a wide belief in the *okuriokami* ("escort wolf") that guided people through the forest at night, and that there were many Shinto wolf shrines. He believes that imported Western ideas changed the Japanese perception of wolves.

As he had in *Summer* Wars, Hosoda offered a portrait of a believable if unconventional Japanese family in *Wolf Children*, and audiences responded enthusiastically. Hosoda won a third Japanese Academy Award for Best Animation Film. At the 2013 Tokyo Anime Awards, *Wolf Children* won Animation of the Year, Art Direction, Character Design, Director, and Screenplay. It also garnered prizes at festivals in Catalonia, Oslo, Amsterdam, and New York.

Audiences and critics outside Japan were equally taken with the film: *Wolf Children* earned a 95 percent Fresh score on Rotten Tomatoes. In the *Daily Telegraph*, Tim Robey said, "Mamoru Hosoda may be the most inspired living animation director in Japan not to be associated with Studio Ghibli…. Hosoda has now outdone himself with a gloriously emotional new picture." Mark Schilling of the *Japan Times* wrote that Hosoda "again delivers moments of sheer exhilaration and delight, as well as making acute observations on everything from the hardships of rural life to the exhaustion of early motherhood."

The critical and box-office success of *Wolf Children* put Studio Chizu on the map in the Japanese animation industry—and ensured that despite the founders' initial plan, the studio would continue producing films.

`TOP **In her dreams, Hana is reunited with her beloved Wolfman.**

RIGHT **As these frames show, Hana maintains the house for herself after Yuki leaves for boarding school. She keeps the Wolfman's driver's license on the family Buddhist altar.**

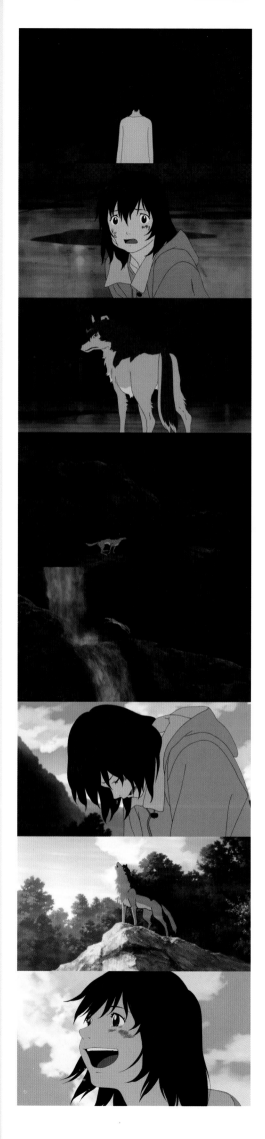

As the typhoon passes, Hana realizes that Ame will leave her to live in the forest as a wolf. The animation drawings and frames underscore his resemblance to his father.

OPPOSITE Ame bids his mother farewell in the school parking lot and climbs the mountain to pursue his destiny. The handsome background painting reflects the boundaries that separate the human and animal worlds.

140 - 16

MARKETING

The merchandise for *Wolf Children* ranged from toys and miniature dioramas to stickers and candy boxes.

OPPOSITE The poster for *Wolf Children*

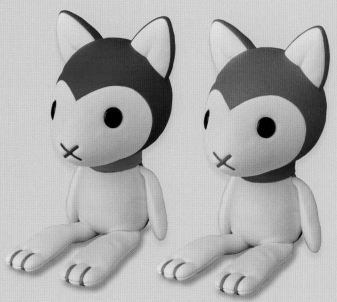

バケモノの子

V. THE BOY
AND THE BEAST

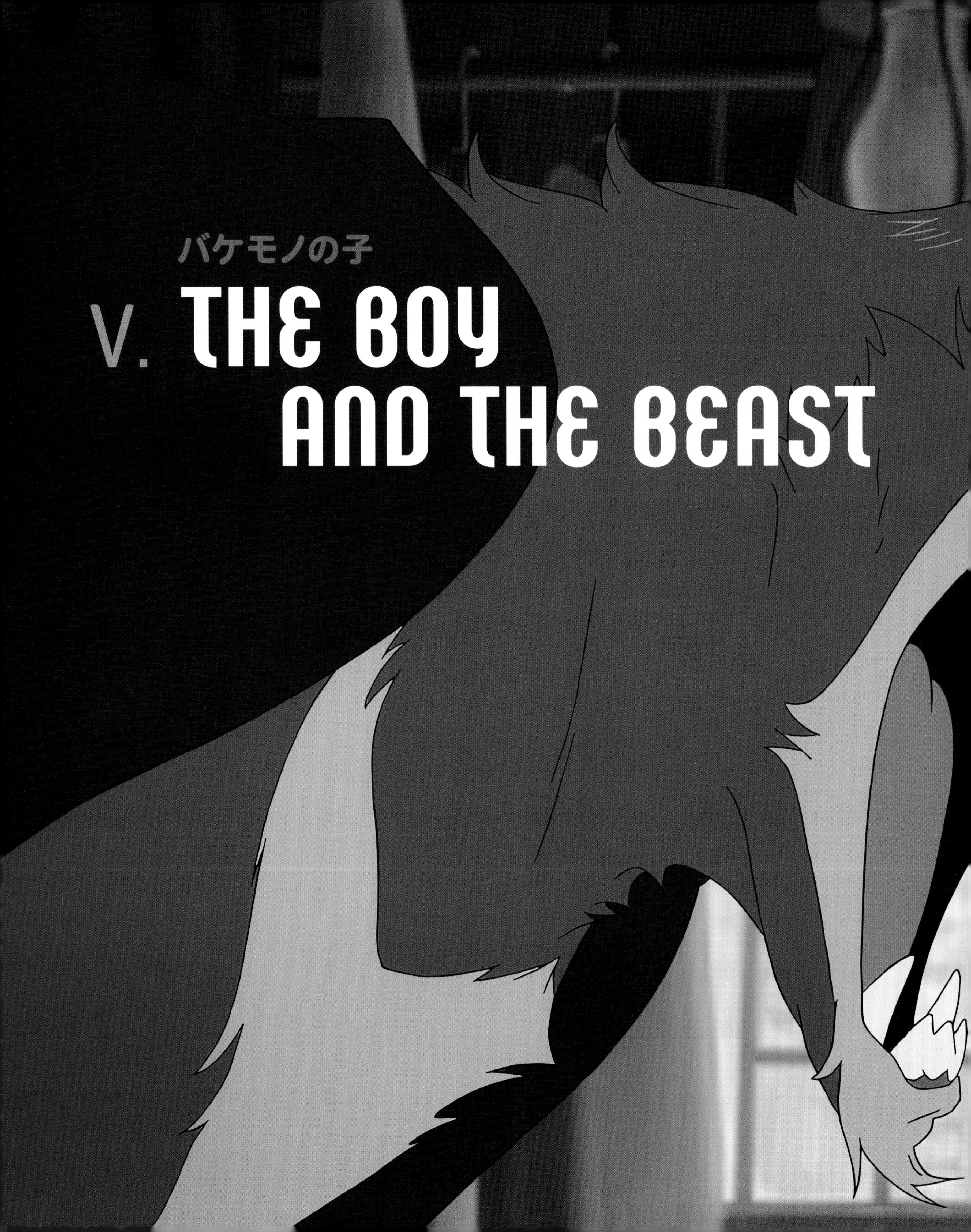

Mamoru Hosoda and Yuichiro Saito had formed Studio

Chizu with a single purpose in mind: to make *Wolf Children*. Saito recalls, "My intention with Studio Chizu was to get through this one movie, and that would be it. Studios can live or die on the success or failure of a single film. If it fails, so be it. If it succeeds, regardless, let's just get through this one movie. I really didn't have any intention of continuing or turning it into a long-term operation. I wasn't as much worried about forming a studio as I was battling with the idea of creating that project."

When *Wolf Children* proved both a critical and a box-office success, it was clear Studio Chizu would continue. For his next film, Hosoda returned to an important theme in his work: how children find the mentors they need to help them grow. He wrote the original story and script for *The Boy and the Beast*, a powerful, visually striking story of an alienated young man's difficult journey to maturity.

"One of the inspirations for *The Boy and the Beast* was Akira Kurosawa's *Yojimbo*, in which each member of two families has a role in their faction," Hosoda says. "When these two factions clash, it gets the audience excited: Each side has their own set of ideals that they bring to the table. It makes for very interesting filmmaking.

"I'm also fascinated with yakuza movies," he continues. "Even *Yojimbo* was about outlaws and thugs. We like the outlaw figure who asserts his presence, who steps outside the bounds of the law and ultimately becomes the hero. The same pattern applies to a lot of Westerns. The younger generation—especially in Japan—probably hasn't been exposed to the old Toei yakuza movies or John Wayne Westerns. I hope that they can experience a similar sensation through *The Boy and the Beast*."

PREVIOUS SPREAD **Kumatetsu and Kyuta fight over teaching methods. Their relationship is more complex than standard master–pupil stories, as each individual is both an instructor and a student.**

ABOVE **These sensitive animation drawings suggest how vulnerable Ren feels when he realizes he's stumbled into the Jutengai.**

During the growth process, children experience turmoil and a sense of things lacking within them. I wanted to depict that not in a dualistic "light and dark" way, but in a positive way, as part of the processes necessary to growing up. Everyone loses sight of their own identity at times, and children live with the burden of their insufficiencies. Adults tend to look for the "right answer," but it's the process that's important. I wanted to scrupulously depict how Ren forms his identity. That's why I made him a character with emotional turmoil in his heart.

—MAMORU HOSODA

After the death of his mother, Ren, a sulky boy of nine, runs away from his stuffy relatives. As he dashes through the crowded streets of Shibuya, he escapes the police and hides in an alley. He's approached by Kumatetsu, an ursine martial arts master who's searching for a student. Ren follows him through a tangle of passageways to the Jutengai, an alternate world of anthropomorphized animals.

"I was in charge of the real world. A lot of what I did was look at Shibuya and re-create it," explains art director Yohei Takamatsu. "Once production designer Anri Jojo had sketched out the worlds, there was a scouting trip to Marrakesh, Morocco. Hosoda and the others mixed what Jojo had created with details from Morocco and merged that into the Jutengai.

"Hosoda first goes on a scouting trip with a very minimal team: He'll find the places he likes, then bring the core staff members on a second trip," he continues. "During these trips, it's all about listening to what Hosoda is saying as we're touring. His words are the biggest key to understanding what the backgrounds should look like. With regards to the backgrounds, Hosoda is a very, very particular director. He has a really strong image of what he wants. Our job as art directors is to close the gap between what's in his head versus what is being output onto paper."

Background paintings of the market in the Jutengai are filled with products its inhabitants use. Some, like the dried toads and lizards, unnerve Kyuta when he first sees them.

The Jutengai was a fantastic world but one that had to feel grounded in reality—and that had to relate to the corresponding human districts of metropolitan Tokyo.

"Jutengai is essentially another Shibuya," says Anri Jojo. "As someone who grew up in Shibuya, I included some landmarks that no longer exist—such as the Tokyo-line train platform and the Gotoh Planetarium—in the designs. We went on the scouting trip to Marrakesh to really capture that disorderly 'open marketplace' feel. I believe that all of us having had the opportunity to witness it firsthand really enhanced the overall expression."

Kumatetsu's extraordinary prowess as a martial artist makes him one of the two candidates to become the next lord of the realm. His rival, the gracious, formal, boar-like Iozen, has a whole cadre of disciples. Kumatetsu desperately needs at least one pupil, but he's impatient, slovenly, and hot-tempered.

Animation director Takaaki Yamashita says, "In the character-design phase, Hosoda and I had a lot of exchanges. Toshiro Mifune in Kurosawa's *Seven Samurai* was a big inspiration for Kumatetsu."

"Kumatetsu's character would fit right into a Kurosawa film," agrees editor Shigeru Nishiyama. "Toei was known for samurai movies that were just sword fights. The composition of those scenes must have felt very close to home for Hosoda, who has roots in Toei. He's definitely a director who can handle action sequences very, very well. Fighting sequences like these are right up his alley."

The combination of human and animal elements in Kumatetsu's final design and his flamboyant movements offer the kind of challenge animators relish. Key animator Hiroyuki Aoyama comments, "I didn't get any scenes with Kumatetsu. I was animating Kaede. I would have liked to take a crack at animating Kumatetsu and making his character full of vitality, but I suppose it just wasn't meant to be."

Ren (whose name Kumatetsu changes to Kyuta when he agrees to take him as a student—it plays off his age: *kyuu*, "nine" in Japanese) is initially repulsed by Kumatetsu's demeanor but attracted to his strength. He agrees to become his student and cleans his grubby quarters, which are strewn with old clothes, dirty dishes, and empty saké bottles. Jojo adds, "Hosoda painted quite the vivid picture: 'Imagine someone living alone, who is a slob by nature but still keeps a fairly stylish wardrobe, and saw a little bit of success in his past—which is when he purchased that designer sofa.'

"I'm quite the slob myself, so it was actually quite easy to create Kumatetsu's home," he concludes with a chuckle.

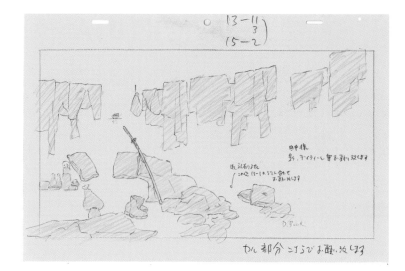

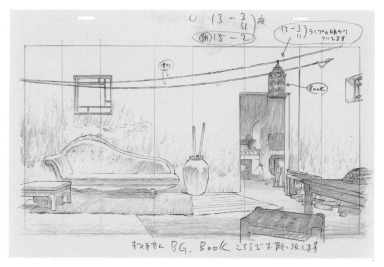

RIGHT, TOP AND SECOND FROM TOP **Two layout** drawings of Kumatetsu's home, the top one showing overlays of dirty garments

RIGHT, SECOND FROM BOTTOM **The painted background of the scene**

RIGHT **A frame from the scene with the characters (and laundry)**

蓮/九太 REN/KYUTA　　　熊徹 KUMATETSU

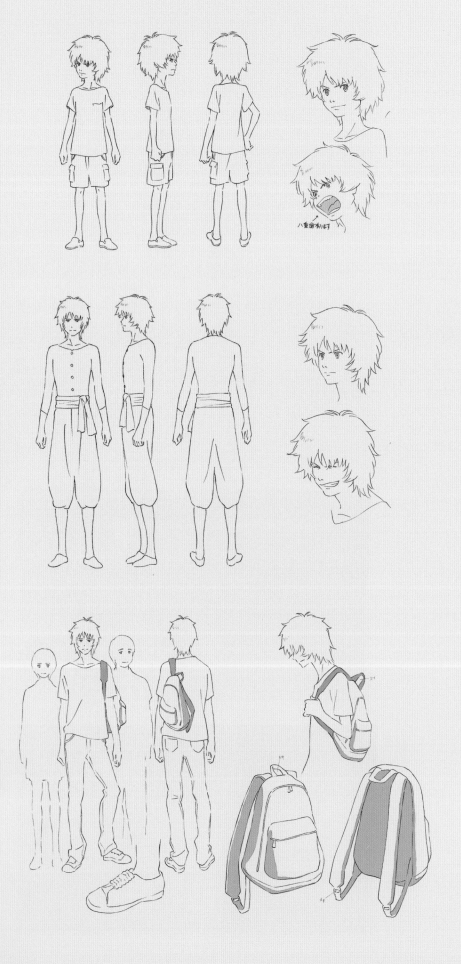

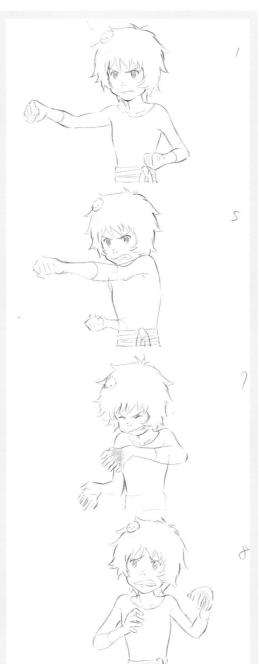

When he begins his training, Kyuta can't even punch a watermelon without hurting his hand.

RIGHT **Four animation drawings**

FAR RIGHT **The same motions in the film**

OPPOSITE **Model sheets of Ren/Kyuta (as an adolescent and a teenager) and Kumatetsu show the characters' proportions, expressions, and details of their attire.**

"One of the images I had in mind for Kumatetsu's character was the bear in the Japanese folktale about a boy named Kintaro [usually translated as "Golden Boy"]," Hosoda explains. "The bear was Kintaro's strongest sumo opponent. If you look at that story, you see the sort of symbolism and rite of passage that a child needs in order to make the transition to adulthood."

The hulking Kumatetsu also recalls a character from a film Hosoda cites as an influence: Disney's *Beauty and the Beast*. Oscar-winning animator and director Glen Keane, who was the supervising animator for Beast, says, "I see Hosoda as standing on the shoulders of what we did in *Beauty and the Beast*. He's taken it to another level and used the symbol of the beast as a way of expressing someone's soul."

At first, Kyuta's training does not go well. Kumatetsu can shatter a huge ceramic vessel with a single punch or kick; Kyuta hurts his hand when he strikes a watermelon. Kumatetsu doesn't know how to teach. His tremendous strength enables him to power through any conflict, but brute strength and gut instinct can't be taught.

OPPOSITE **Hosoda's storyboards of Kumatetsu and Kyuta's dispute about raw eggs over rice for breakfast**

ABOVE **Tatara, the sardonic monkey, and Hyakushubo, the gentle porcine monk, look on as Kumatetsu and teenage Kyuta squabble over breakfast, in an animation drawing.**

Then Kyuta has an epiphany: As he washes dishes, he overhears Kumatetsu gloating when he beats his sardonic monkey friend Tatara at cards. Kyuta has watched Kumatetsu so carefully, he knows every step he'll take. That's why Kumatetsu can't beat Iozen: He always makes the same moves. Iozen knows what to expect. The next morning, when Kumatetsu goes through his regular warm-up, Kyuta is ready. He anticipates his teacher's movements, tripping him up and delivering the coup de grâce with a broom.

Kyuta never forms a touchy-feely *Karate Kid* Daniel-san/Mr. Miyagi bond with his mentor. They argue over everything from breakfast (raw eggs broken over rice) to Kumatetsu's teaching skills. As they bicker and shout, they learn and grow and develop a grudging affection for each other, a process Hosoda captures by juxtaposing slapstick, action, and reflective sequences.

During the sparring and training, they often trade roles as student and teacher. Kyuta instructs Kumatetsu in a key principle of martial arts combat: Analyze your opponent's moves and use them against him. "Let my movements tell you what to do: You follow me!" When Kumatetsu charges in without thinking, Kyuta whacks him with a wooden sword. At the same time, Kyuta learns how to throw a punch and wield a sword.

THIS SPREAD **Breakfast** with Kyuta and Kumatetsu quickly devolves into yet another shouting match, in these vivid animation drawings.

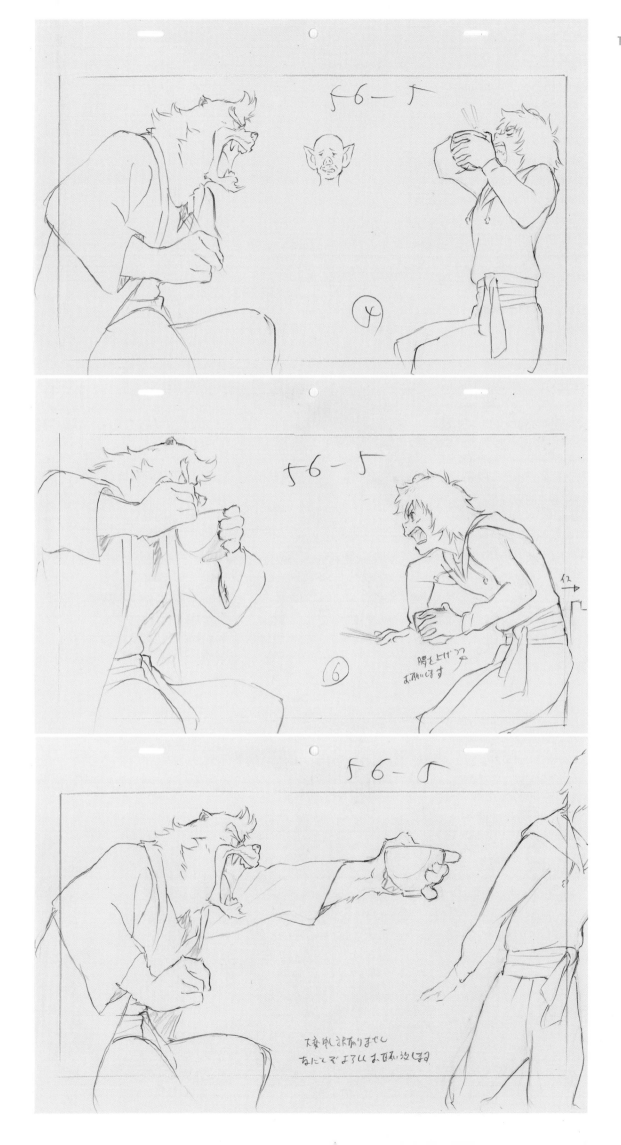

"We studied movements from sumo and *iaido*, as well as many other martial arts and combat techniques to animate those scenes, but more than that, we studied the spirit of those arts," Hosoda notes.

Kyuta's training takes place under the watchful eyes of Tatara and Hyakushubo, a gentle, porcine monk. They provide a running commentary, marking Kyuta's progress and observing how the relationship between the boy and his teacher shifts to accommodate his growing skill. When Tatara says of Kumatetsu, "Following isn't exactly something that comes naturally to him," Hyakushubo counters, "He's never had anyone to follow but himself."

David Silverman, the director of *The Simpsons Movie*, comments, "I love the way Hosoda treats the monkey and the pig. They're broadly designed characters, but they're played with such human mannerisms and humor. *The Boy and the Beast* contains some very serious elements and it's very dramatic; the climax is incredibly scary. But the film is also very comic. When people try to do more serious animation, they often get deadly serious. They forget about having some comedic charm to enliven and enrich the characters and to connect the characters to the audience."

"For *Wolf Children*, we were going for realism, but with *The Boy and the Beast*, we didn't want the characters to feel too bestial," explains costume supervisor Daisuke Iga. "During the brainstorming, we tapped into anthropomorphized characters I'd seen in Disney movies and other animated films. We drew from those masters while considering how it would look if these characters were placed in a Hosoda film. It was a long process.

RIGHT **Kyuta uses the predictability that weakens Kumatetsu as a martial artist to outmaneuver him in these animation drawings.**

OPPOSITE **The sequence in the film**

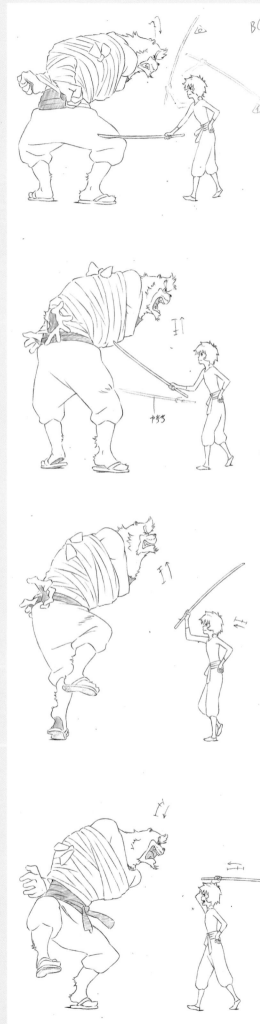
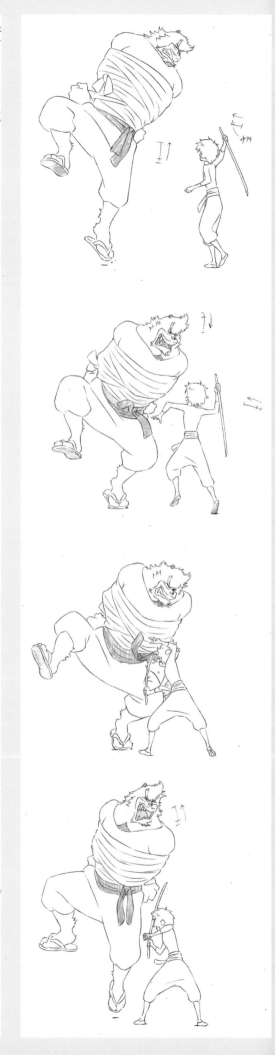

The master and the student switch roles. Kyuta teaches Kumatetsu a key element of martial arts combat: Learn to read your opponent's moves.

OPPOSITE AND ABOVE A series of animation drawings

RIGHT A frame from the film

"When I design characters and wardrobe with Hosoda, we spend an immense amount of time in the discussion phase going through what each character is like—what's their upbringing, their background," he adds. "You can naturally extend that to how they might be dressed in different phases in their life without losing a sense of that character."

Over the course of eight years, Kyuta grows strong and adept. He begins as the skinny kid anyone can bully, but he becomes an assured fighter who's a match for Iozen's younger son Jiromaru. At the same time, Kumatetsu becomes more disciplined and focused. Their shared progress astonishes Hyakushubo and Tatara—and even the rabbit Lord of the Jutengai, who notes, "Kumatetsu has grown more than the boy has.... Which is the master and which the apprentice?"

"I think that parents and teachers have historically taken a 'top-down' approach to raising children, but these days I suspect it's become more mutual growth," Hosoda reflects. "Parents and teachers today can be considered imperfect; they and their children need to mature together. I used the relationship between Kumatetsu and Kyuta to express my wish for children to encounter different people whom they can call their 'teachers of choice,' people who help them mature into adults. Simultaneously, I wanted to show adults how wonderful it is we don't have to just look back on those bygone days when we were 'growing up'—we can keep on growing. It may be impossible for someone to become a perfected, flawless being, but if they use the power of the connection Kumatetsu and Kyuta share, flawed people may be able to surpass perfect ones."

Tiring of the Jutengai, Kyuta revisits the human world; he befriends Kaede, a smart, shy girl he protects from bullying classmates. In return, she helps him read *Moby-Dick*: They meet when he asks her how to read 鯨 (*kujira*, the kanji for "whale"; "white whale" in the English release). Kyuta's traditional education had come to a halt during his eight years in the Jutengai; although he's intelligent and curious, his reading and math skills are rusty. Impressed by his desire to learn, Kaede encourages and tutors him.

At the climax of the film, Kumatetsu duels Iozen to become the next Lord of the Jutengai. Although the match begins badly, Kyuta arrives in time to coach his master to victory. Iozen concedes as the crowd of beasts cheer the victor. Then Iozen's adopted human son Ichirohiko treacherously stabs Kumatetsu. The Lord and other beasts are right to fear "the darkness that dwells within the human heart," represented by a black-rimmed void in the youths' chests.

The sardonic Tatara and gentle Hyakushubo
watch as Kyuta trains Kumatetsu.

LEFT AND OPPOSITE The animation drawings
for the scene establish the characters' poses.

BELOW Stills from the scene

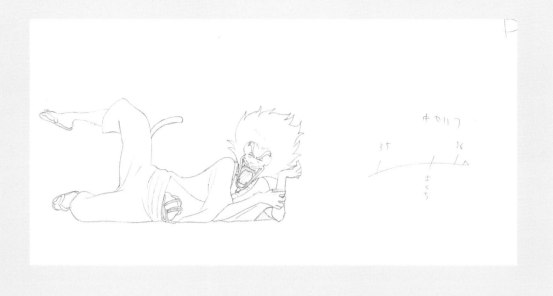

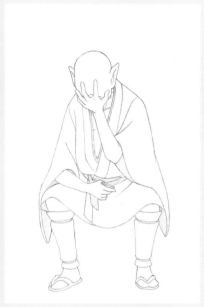

スタジオ地図

58-3　原図村 ②/2

Kyuta must defeat Ichirohiko—and the menacing emptiness that threatens to engulf both their hearts. Ichirohiko flees to the human world; Kyuta follows, pausing to bid Kaede goodbye. The epic battle between the human warriors evokes *Moby-Dick*: In a spectacular combination of drawn animation and CG, Ichirohiko assumes the form of the great white whale. His black silhouette glides ominously beneath the glowing neon of the iconic Shibuya Scramble Crossing, then bursts into the starry night sky above the Yoyogi Daiichi Gym as a three-dimensional blue-white monster.

"There are two battle sequences where music required a lot of thought. The first is in the town square where the audience surrounds Kumatetsu and Iozen as they fight," recalls composer Masakatsu Takagi. "In a modern, metropolitan sense, it's like a rap battle or a dance battle. It's very festival-like.

"On the other hand, there's Kyuta's fight with the whale," he continues. "One thing I was 100 percent sure about in that scene was that Kyuta grew throughout the battle. It reminded me a lot of *Dragon Quest*: You have the music that plays during the battle and the music that plays after battle when the characters level up. I was trying to create those two vibes in a single track."

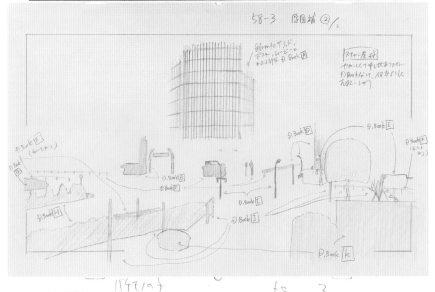

スタジオ地図   S. 58 C. 3   TIME(+)

FROM TOP LEFT **A reference photograph, a page of notes from the assistant director, a layout drawing, the background, and a final frame of the famous Shibuya Scramble Crosswalk—the busiest pedestrian intersection in the world**

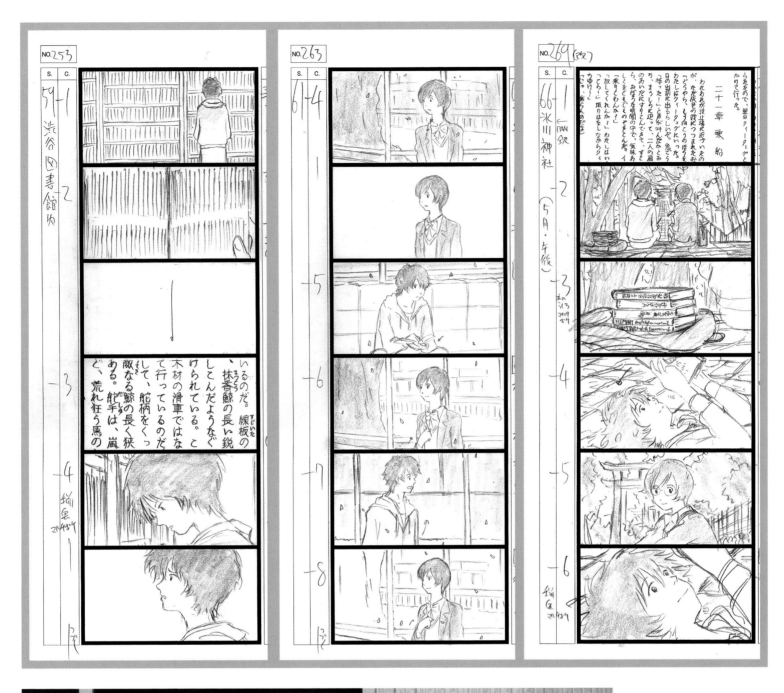

ABOVE Hosoda's storyboards show Kyuta is eager to learn—but daunted by his unfamiliarity with some of the complex Kanji characters.

LEFT Kaede comes to his aid.

Kyuta's encouragement inspires Kumatetsu to defeat Iozen in their battle to determine the next ruler of the Jutengai in Hosoda's dramatic storyboards.

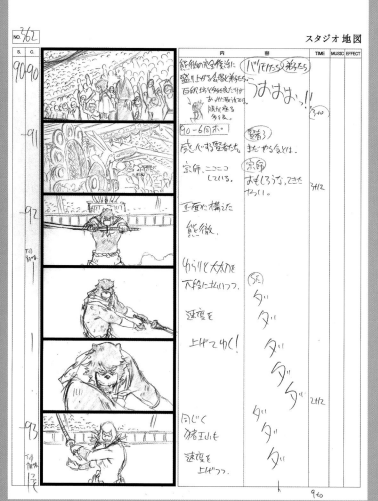

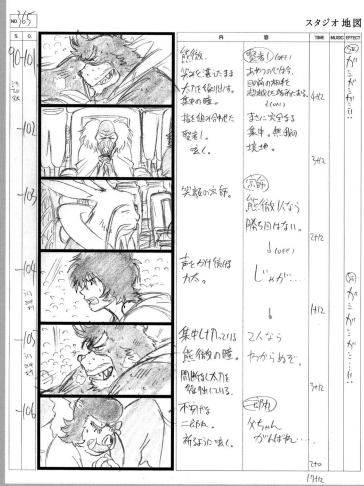

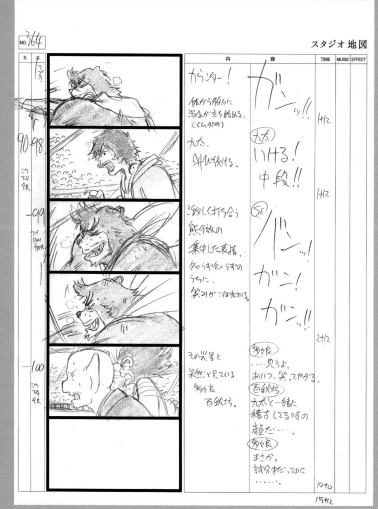

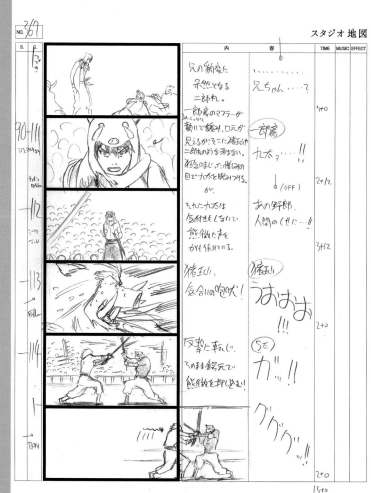

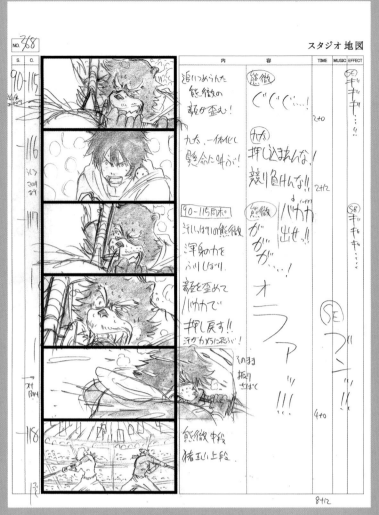

NO. 368　スタジオ地図

S.C.	内容	TIME	MUSIC	EFFECT
90-115	追いつめられた熊徹の顔が歪む！ （熊徹）ぐぐぐ……！！	2+0		ギリギリ…
-116	九太、一体化し懸命に叫ぶ！ （九太）押し込まれんな！！競り負けんな！！	2+12		
-117	90-115同ポ それにはゲリの熊徹 渾身の力をふりしぼり、顔を歪めて（熊徹）バカが…ががが……！			ギリギリ…
	顔を歪めてバカで押し戻す!! （熊徹）オラァッ!!!			SB出せ!!
		4+0		ドン!!
-118	熊徹 中段　猪王山 上段			
		8+12		

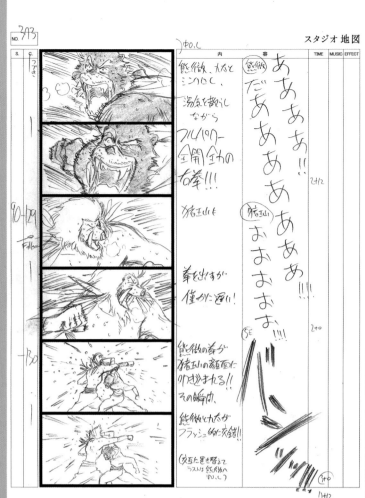

NO. 373　スタジオ地図

S.C.	内容	TIME	MUSIC	EFFECT
-1	熊徹、九太とシンクロし、湯気を散らしながらフルパワー全開全力の右拳!!! （熊徹）ああああ!!!だああああああああ!!!	2+12		
90-129	猪王山も（猪王山）おおおおおおお!!!!			
-1	拳を出すが僅かに遅い!			
-130	熊徹の拳が猪王山の顔面に叩きつけられる!! その瞬間、熊徹と九太がフラッシュ的に交錯!!			バン
-1	(交互に置き換えてラストは熊徹へ　やく)	2+0		ツツ!!!
		14+12		

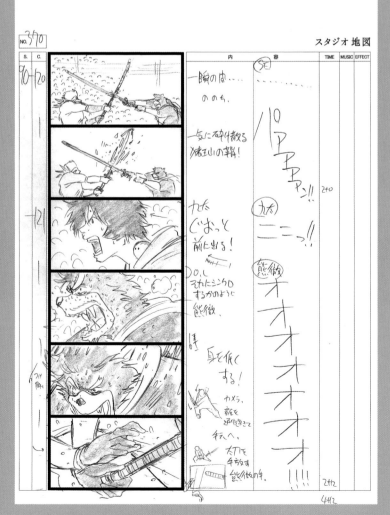

NO. 370　スタジオ地図

S.C.	内容	TIME	MUSIC	EFFECT
90-120	一瞬の時…… ののち、			SE ……
-1	一気に石砕け散る猪王山の鞘!			ハァァ…ッ!!
-121	（九太）ぐおっと前に出る! （九太）ニーッ!!	2+0		
-1	O.L それと シンクロするかのように熊徹、 （熊徹）オオオオオ!!!!			
	身を低くする! カメラ、顔を通り過ぎて太刀へ、太刀を手ちらす熊徹の手			
		2+12		
		4+12		

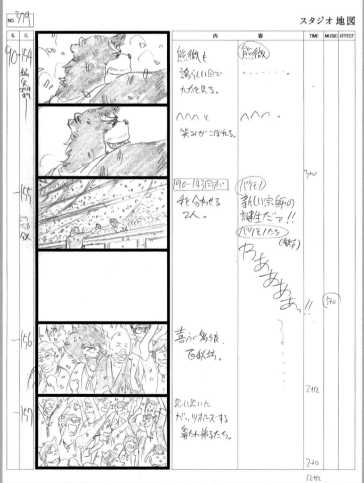

NO. 379　スタジオ地図

S.C.	内容	TIME	MUSIC	EFFECT
90-154	熊徹も誇らしい目で九太を見る。 （熊徹）……			
	へへへと笑いがこぼれる。 （熊徹）へへへ			
-155	90-143同ポ 手を合わせる2人。 （バケモノ）新しい宗師の誕生だァ!! （バケモノたち）うわあああああ…!!	3+0		
		2+12		
-156	喜ぶ多々良、百秋坊。			
-157	感い込んだガッツポーズする熊徹の弟子たち。	2+0		
		12+12		

155

THIS SPREAD **Kumatetsu** scores an upset victory over Iozen—with a little help from Kyuta.

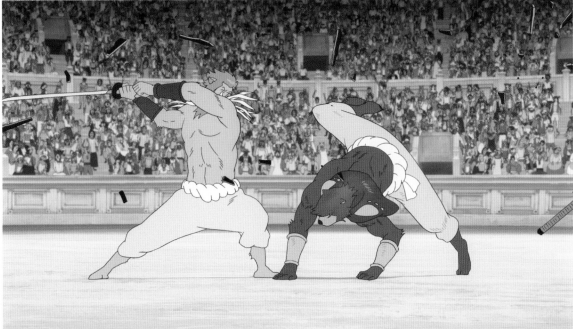

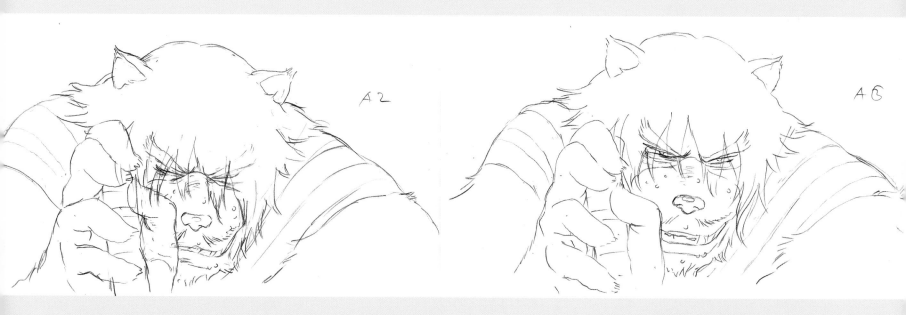

Mortally wounded by Ichirohiko, Kumatetsu
demands the right to reincarnate so he can aid
Kyuta: "I may be a fool and a bum and slob, but
I'm going to help him be strong!"

ABOVE LEFT AND OPPOSITE **Powerful**
animation drawings capture the character's
pain—and his determination.

ABOVE **Frames of the same scenes**

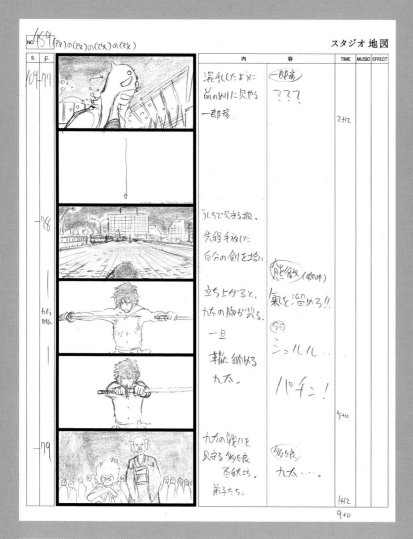

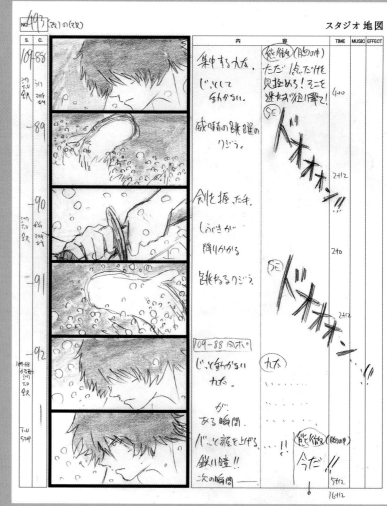

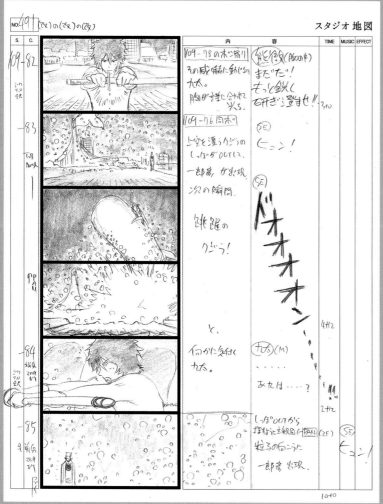

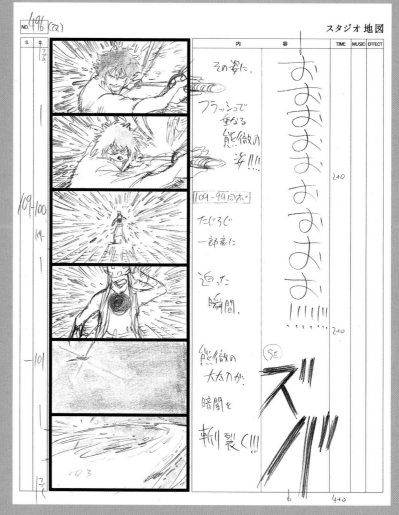

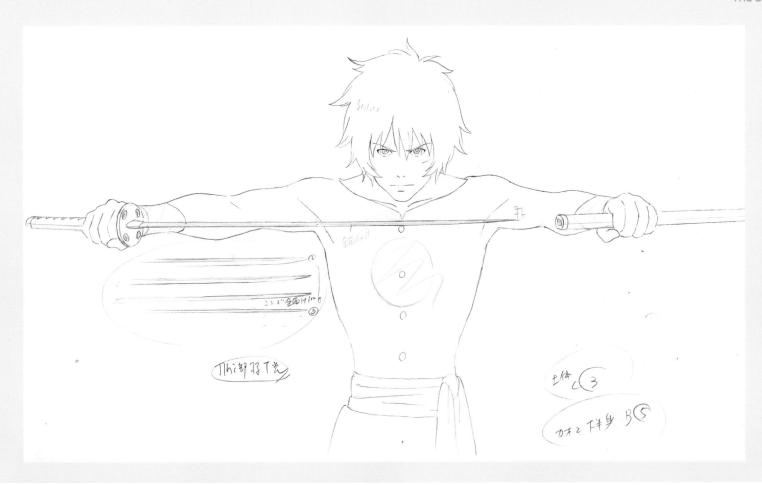

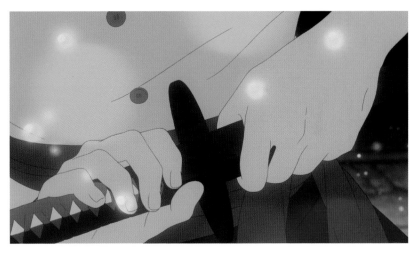

Masato Matsushima, a researcher at the Tokyo National Museum, notes that Hosoda emphasizes the scale and power of the whale by not showing the creature's entire form at one time and by contrasting its size with the diminutive figure of Kyuta standing at the corner of the screen. He compares the sequence to ukiyo-e artist Utagawa Kuniyoshi's celebrated print *Miyamoto Musashi Subduing the Whale*.

The blade that embodies Kumatetsu heals the void in Kyuta's chest. The love and support of Kumatetsu and Kaede give Kyuta the strength and resolve to defeat his foe, not by killing him, but by conquering the inner demons that would have destroyed them both. Virtue triumphs over vengeance, understanding over hatred.

TOP **Kyuta draws his sword in this dramatic animation drawing.**

ABOVE **Two frames from the scene**

OPPOSITE **Four pages of Hosoda's storyboard of the climactic battle between Kyuta and Ichirohiko, who assumes the form of a great white whale**

OPPOSITE **Kyuta prepares to strike, in an animation drawing and a frame from the sequence.**

THIS PAGE **The reincarnated Kumatetsu mirrors his pose and lends Kyuta his strength, in an animation drawing and in a final frame.**

バケモノの子

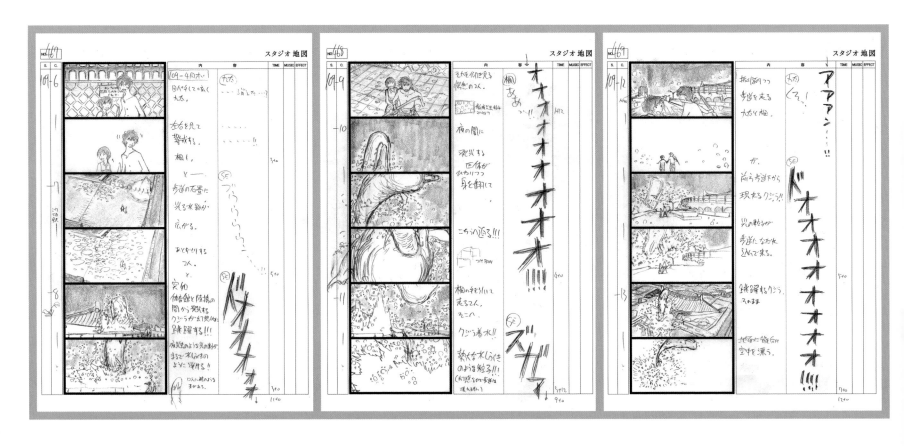

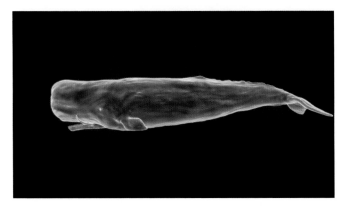

OPPOSITE, TOP Three pages of Hosoda's storyboard of the whale's attack

OPPOSITE, MIDDLE *Miyamoto Musashi and the Whale Off the Coast of Hizen* by Utagawa Kuniyoshi (1798–1861)

OPPOSITE, BOTTOM Two images of the CG whale

LEFT A background painting of the Yoyogi Daichi Gymnasium

BELOW The computer-generated whale and effects to suggest the water it emerges from

BOTTOM The completed image

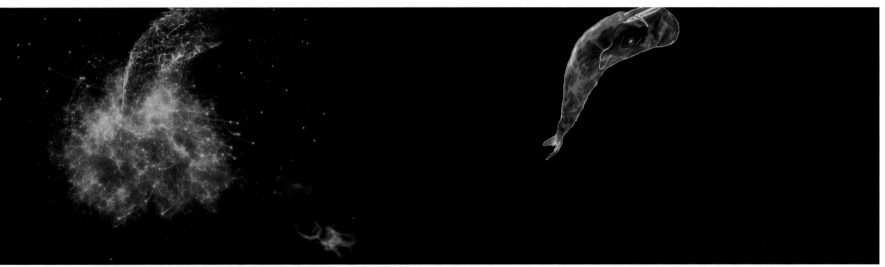

Hosoda, who read Melville as an adolescent, explains: "Kaede says, 'Ichirohiko is fighting the very darkness—the "beast"—within himself.' I cited *Moby-Dick* in the film to show that it's humans who are beastlike, and beasts who are humane. The whale is a symbol of human desire, so it's highly symbolic for a whale to swim through Shibuya, a human city steeped in desire. The mixture of ugliness and beauty is a key here, so the whale is depicted in a dreamlike, beautiful way."

Pixar art director Ralph Eggleston comments, "Although the whale is CG, it's really unified with the overall visual. That's not an easy thing to do. The most difficult thing to do is to beat the literalness out of the CG imagery. Hosoda has this picture in his head, and he just does it."

His apprenticeship completed, Kyuta returns to the human world. He establishes a relationship with his biological father, whom he never knew, and pursues his education. Although he would never touch a sword again, he remains a great swordsman. Hyakushubo notes, "In his soul is a sword called Kumatetsu. No one else can say that." It's Hosoda's metaphor for the strength people derive from beloved mentors who have passed away. Tatara adds, "He can overcome any obstacle that stands in his path because he won't have to do it alone."

Looking back on the production, Saito reflects, "Up to *The Boy and the Beast*, my role was like a tailor: look at the overall budget and try to figure out how to make the pieces fit. I was known—and complimented—in the industry as the producer who never went into the red. During *The Boy and the Beast*, I would show the budget to Hosoda and check with him. I think he let it go in one ear and out the other."

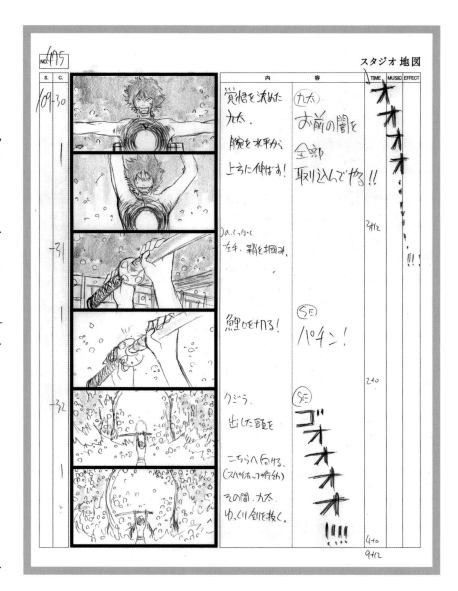

Kyuta's real foe is not the whale or Ichirohiko, but the darkness hidden in his own heart, represented as a gaping void.

ABOVE RIGHT **Hosoda's storyboards**

RIGHT **Two frames of the climactic confrontation**

OPPOSITE, TOP **Another storyboard panel**

OPPOSITE, MIDDLE AND BOTTOM **Two frames show Ichirohiko attempting to confuse Kyuta.**

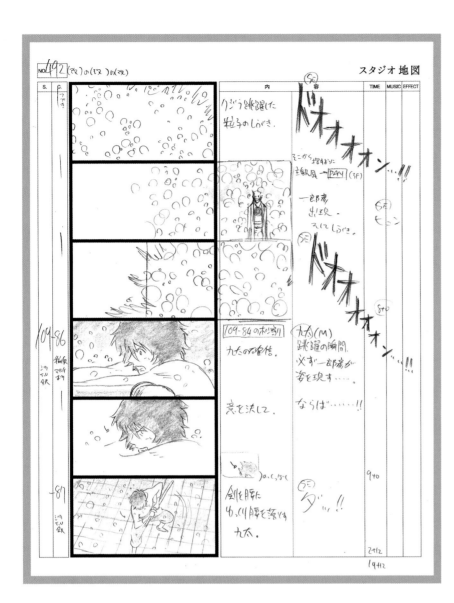

The Boy and the Beast won Hosoda his fourth Japanese Academy Award for Best Animation Film and received the Japan Movie Critics Award.

The film drew praise from critics in Europe and America. Simon Abrams of RogerEbert.com said, "Hosoda's knack for choreographing big action set pieces and quiet dialogue moments really makes his latest feature an emotionally rewarding crowd-pleaser. Almost all animated filmmakers appeal to their pint-sized audience's emotions, but few are able to keep adult viewers equally engaged." *Variety*'s Peter Debruge concluded, "Hosoda orchestrates this chaos with a poetic sense of what each must do for his own salvation, giving the title characters their respective whopper-unities to prove themselves as the most heroic boy and beast who've ever lived."

The "big action set piece," the battle between the boy and the whale, showcases Hosoda's skill at blending drawn and CG animation in striking, imaginative ways. "I want to demonstrate the possibilities of animation by using pioneering visual expressions, by depicting familiar motifs that anyone can identify with in a fictitious world completely different from our own," he concludes. "People often ask me, 'Why don't you make purely CG films?' But in the art world, nobody says, 'Oil paints are old, and the digital art on your tablet is the new thing.' I don't think the techniques you use are important. What's important is your art itself: That's what moves people emotionally."

スタジオ 地図　　　　　　　S. 113　C. 5　　　TIME(+)

113-4

The victorious Kyuta prepares to depart the Jutengai.

TOP Three frames from the sequence

ABOVE, SECOND FROM TOP The Lord of the Jutengai and some of the leaders Kyuta and Kumatetsu visited look on, in this layout drawing.

ABOVE Tatara and Hyakushubo proudly watch their friend, in another layout drawing.

RIGHT, SECOND FROM TOP AND ABOVE Kaede surprises Kyuta and happily flrourishes his college application, in two additional animation drawings.

RIGHT Animator Hiroyuki Aoyama comments, "There's a lot of performance in the storyboard. Hosoda-san will give verbal feedback, then he'll re-show us the storyboards and really dial in the performance."

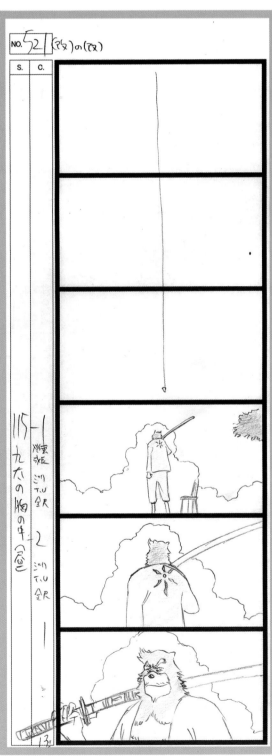

Although Kyuta may never again draw a sword, Kumatetsu will always be with him, to help him overcome whatever obstacles he may face in life.

ABOVE Two frames from the film

LEFT Hosoda's storyboards of the scene. Kyuta keeps his late mother's picture on his desk.

MARKETING

Character merchandise from the film included plates, pins, picture frames, candy boxes, and frames of film to hang on cell phones or backpacks.

OPPOSITE The poster for *The Boy and the Beast*

未来のミライ

VI. MIRAI

Although more intimate in scale than *The Boy and the*

Beast, *Mirai* (*Mirai no Mirai*, or "Mirai of the Future," in Japanese) is a nostalgic, charming film that incorporates elements of Hosoda's earlier work: time travel from *The Girl Who Leapt Through Time*; trips to alternate worlds from *Summer Wars* and *The Boy and the Beast*; the struggles of well-meaning but overextended parents from *Wolf Children*; a child's search for an appropriate mentor from *Wolf Children* and *The Boy and the Beast*.

Mirai was inspired by the birth of Hosoda's daughter, also named "Mirai." "My films come from my personal experiences," Hosoda explains. "With *Wolf Children*, my mother had passed away; I wrote it thinking about how I was raised. *The Boy and the Beast* was based on my own father and fatherhood. I'm an only child, which is rare for my generation; that's why I was inspired when my son welcomed a baby sister and became an older brother. Kun is exactly like my son, who was three at the time."

Hosoda's son also suggested the key element of interacting with relatives from the past and future: "Every day, I ask my son about his dreams from the previous night. Usually they're about trains, his favorite toy, but one day he said, 'I met Mirai. I met Mirai when she was bigger, like when she was older.' I got jealous, because I wanted to meet her when she's bigger. I started to imagine what she would be like, what kind of woman she would grow up to be. That's how the whole story came about."

PREVIOUS SPREAD **An older Mirai tickles Kun, reducing him to spasms of giggles.**

ABOVE **Kun, the teenage Mirai, and the human form of Yukko sneak into the house to put away the dolls of the Imperial Court.**

OPPOSITE **A preliminary visualization of the interior of Kun's family's house shows how his trains have taken over the living room.**

"The way human lives repeat and overlap is similar to the way the cycles of nature repeat and continue forever," he reflects. "I wanted to portray the cycle of life and the magnificent loop made from the fabric of our lives through the story of a house, a yard, and an ordinary family."

General producer Nozomu Takahashi adds, "I was kind of the Nippon TV representative, but my actual role was more their back-up inside Nippon TV. I told Hosoda, 'Make anything you want, and we won't say anything about it.' I also told the Studio Chizu people to make what Hosoda wants. Whether it succeeds or fails, he'll take something away and apply it in the future."

Four-year-old Kun is the happily spoiled son of a modern Japanese couple. His mother is a busy editor; his father, a self-employed architect who designed their multilevel Western-style house in Yokohama. When his mother comes home from the hospital with a new baby sister, Kun is initially curious: He watches the baby's tiny hand curl around his finger. But when he realizes she's a usurper who's replaced him as the center of attention, Kun fusses, tries to hit his sister with a toy train, and decorates her face with animal cookies.

"Hosoda embraces the parts of life you find the most frustrating and the most wonderful at the same time," says Oscar-winning animator Glen Keane. "I'll never forget the scene of Kun touching the baby's fingers. The exploration of the wonder of a baby's fingers.

I'm not the father in the story. I am more like Kun. Everyone was a four-year-old once. I think what Kun experiences in the story—his identity crisis, finding a way to accept others—are things everyone will experience at some point in their lives. That includes me. Kun is inside all of us.

—MAMORU HOSODA

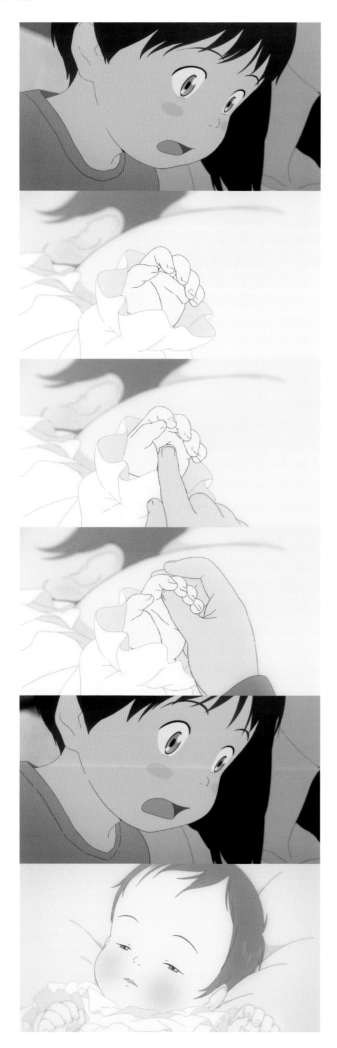

Animating gentle. Animating tender. Animating discovery. Hosoda does that so well without trying to make it more than it is: He just lets it speak for itself. Then the little brother who touched her fingers looks at the baby and smacks her on the head with his train. That's exactly the way kids are, and Hosoda doesn't shy away from it."

Takayuki Hamada, whose animation of Mirai's fingers impressed Keane, had recently become a father during the production. He was able to observe a baby's movements closely and capture them in his drawings.

"People say my stories are about families; I like to think I tell stories about children and how they grow up," replies Hosoda. "I want to make movies about various situations in life. By using animation to tell stories that haven't already been told, I hope to contribute to the art of cinema. In *Mirai*, I wanted to showcase the importance of the little moments in everyday life. I think I came up with a different type of movie that people seem to like."

After being scolded and—he feels—neglected by his parents, the unhappy Kun seeks refuge under the sheltering oak tree in the garden. There he experiences a series of surreal adventures with members of his family, beginning with an elegant young man who laments losing *his* position at the center of the family—to Kun. It's Yukko, the dog, the first character to show Kun the world from a different point of view.

"When you first meet the prince, you think, maybe he's the spirit of the house or something," says David Silverman, the director of *The Simpsons Movie*. "No, he's a dog, who used to be the king of the household. I love that persona because he's just a dog! But he really has a sense of dignity, like royalty."

Kun's next visitor is a teenage Mirai, who becomes his younger and older sister simultaneously. She tickles him and persuades him and Yukko to put away his mother's elaborate set of dolls, fearing a superstition that leaving them out would delay meeting her future husband. (The dolls, which represent the Imperial court in Heian-era robes, are traditionally

ABOVE Oscar-winning animator Glen Keane discuses the scene of baby Mirai trying to grasp Kun's finger with Hosoda at Animation Is Film in Los Angeles.

LEFT A puzzled Kun contemplates his new sister, unaware of how her arrival will upset his life.

displayed on March 3, *Hinamatsuri*, "Girl's Day" or "Doll's Day" in English.) Masakatsu Takagi's jagged piano score emphasizes the nervousness of the three conspirators as they try to wrap up the fragile dolls without attracting the distracted father's notice—even when the Emperor's baton gets stuck to the seat of his pants.

"Hosoda occasionally does very tricky things, and that sequence was one of the trickiest," recalls editor Shigeru Nishiyama. "We employed a lot of quick scenes, and then the scenes that needed to be extended were extended. I don't know if Hosoda enjoyed putting together that sequence, but I did."

"This movie does not follow the normal three-act structure, but a five-act/five-episode structure," Hosoda explains. "Each act features a member of the family: Yukko, Mirai, the mom and the dad, the great-grandfather, Kun. There is also an intertwining storyline about the family tree, symbolized by the tree in their yard."

During his explorations, Kun discovers his father was a skinny boy who had trouble learning to ride a bike. His mother was a rambunctious little girl whose delight in making messes belies her lectures about putting away his toys. Kun learns her trick of placing a note in her mother's shoe to request something: She asked for a cat; he wants a bicycle.

"If this were a time-travel movie, the music should reflect the periods accurately," says composer Masakatsu Takagi. "But very early in development, Hosoda showed me a video on his iPhone of his son playing. To an adult, the scene looked like a small tree maybe waist high and a little bit of grass, nothing too special. But he was filming it from the kid's perspective so the grass looked like a field, the tree like a forest. The music reflected a conscious choice to represent the world from Kun's perspective."

ABOVE RIGHT Kun awaits his mother's return in Hosoda's storyboard and frames from the film. Kun's small, ordinary actions of blowing on the window and drawing in the condensation quickly establish him as a believable little boy.

RIGHT Composer Masakatsu Takagi recalls, "Early in the project's development, Hosoda-san showed me a video on his iPhone, of his son playing. If you are an adult, the scene is just a small tree and a little bit of grass. But he was filming from the son's perspective, so the tree is a forest. It led to the idea of viewing things from the kid's perspective. The music reflects a conscious choice to represent the world from Kun's perspective."

太田家
THE OTA
FAMILY

おとうさんの身長

くんちゃんの身長

OPPOSITE Models sheets show the relative size of the characters, as well as details like the pattern on Kun's shoes, where the birthmark appears on Mirai's right wrist.

LEFT AND BELOW Kun meets a regal young man who is actually Yukko the dog—who lost his place at the center of the household when Kun was born.

BOTTOM Hosoda's storyboards of their meeting

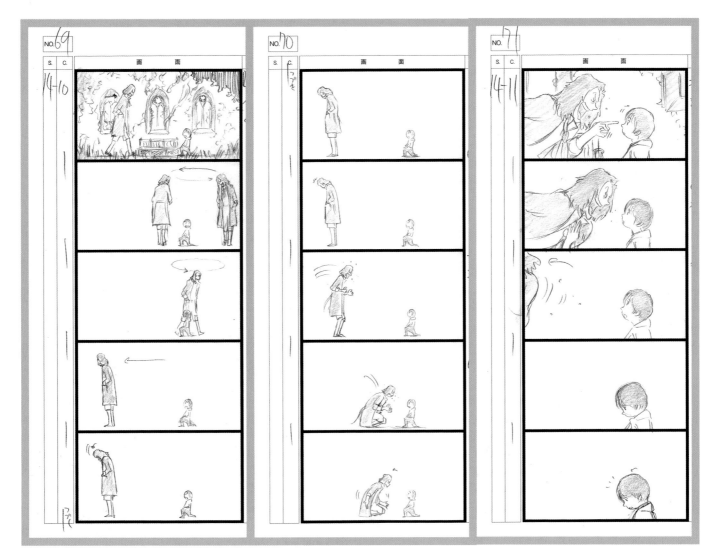

Kun takes out his frustrations by decorating his sister's face with animal cookies while his absent-minded father focuses on his work.

BOTTOM LEFT Hosoda's storyboards of Kun's mischief.

BOTTOM RIGHT An older Mirai confronts Kun.

ABOVE AND LEFT **Mirai and Yukko** try to get the Girls' Day doll set put away without disturbing the father, in these animation drawings.

BELOW **Hosoda's** storyboards of the scene

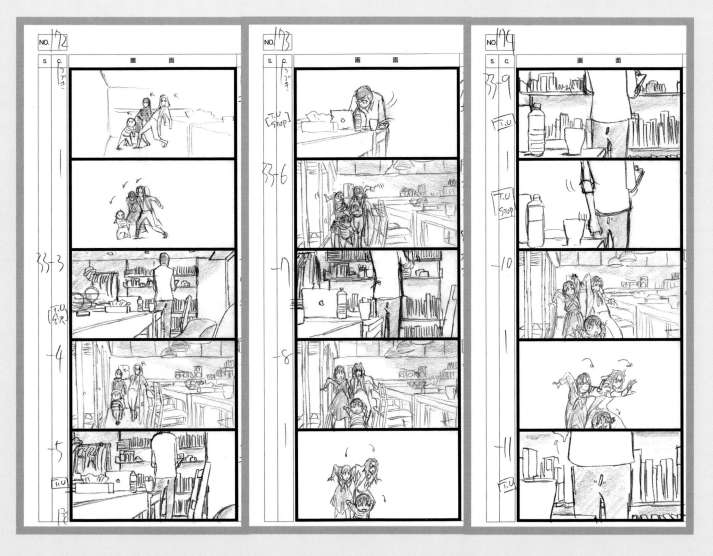

OPPOSITE PAGE **Mirai, Kun, and Yukko** try to get the emperor doll's baton that is stuck to the seat of their father's pants, in three animation drawings and three frames from the film.

THIS PAGE Teenage Mirai struggles to maintain her balance and her silence while sneaking up on her father.

The tree in the courtyard symbolizes Kun's family tree and the bonds its members share.

RIGHT A layout drawing, from the fantasy sequence where Kun meets the future Mirai, shows tropical foliage growing around the tree in the courtyard.

BELOW
A background painting shows the tree in the courtyard as it might appear several years later, when Kun is a high school student.

When Kun sees the other boys in Negishi Forest Park riding without training wheels, he demands his father remove them from his new bike. But Kun doesn't know how to balance; he keeps falling over. Frustrated and bruised, he tearfully declares he'll never touch the bike again. His father, distracted by the crying baby, doesn't know how to help Kun with this challenge.

Kun's next adventure introduces him to his great-grandfather, a dashing man who rode horses and motorcycles despite a war injury that left him with a permanent limp. It's a magical sequence, bathed in a golden glow that underscores its nostalgic warmth. The artists searched the Web for old photographs of Yokohama for reference, plotting out the motorcycle's route on old maps.

"Hosoda had a very strong vision of what he wanted in that scene: It took many trials and errors before we got the final OK," explains art director Yohei Takamatsu. "He said there should be some areas in the backgrounds that don't have any paint at all. That's the level of the exposure he wanted. As it transitions into evening, we added a little bit of yellows and then some oranges. When you take whites, yellows, and oranges, they give a golden feel to the ambience."

"We all have some faint memory or vision of a much older male figure, your dad or your grandfather, teaching you how to ride a bicycle or sitting you on their motorcycle," says Hosoda. "When you're a little kid, riding these vehicles really instills this unique sense of joy. So you project a very cool figure onto whomever that older male might be. Maybe dads don't ride motorbikes anymore or maybe father figures aren't as needed in modern society. But the nostalgia for that type of relationship stays in our heart."

His great-grandfather's lessons—look ahead, not down when you ride anything, and, more importantly, not to be afraid of the challenges of a new experience—enable Kun to master the bicycle and win the friendship of the other boys. His parents are pleased but puzzled at his sudden progress.

"The great-grandfather character definitely left a strong impression," comments animation director Hiroyuki Aoyama. "I wouldn't say that resulted from the animation as much as from Hosoda's story and storyboards. It was hard not to feel for that very attractive character."

"That was one of the more challenging sequences of the movie, and we had to edit to the music," adds Nishiyama. "The first assemblies didn't match the music at all, so we extended a lot of the scenes and played around with the visuals. The edits had to be very, very carefully chosen. Kun is talking to someone who passed on a long time ago, but we wanted to convey a connection that transcends reality. It was a huge challenge for us."

LEFT, TOP AND SECOND FROM TOP **Kun's dashing great-grandfather, who teaches him courage—and how to ride anything, from a horse to a two-wheeler**

ABOVE LEFT AND LEFT **Background paintings of Yokohama decades ago**

The background artists researched old photographs of Yokohama to depict each setting accurately.

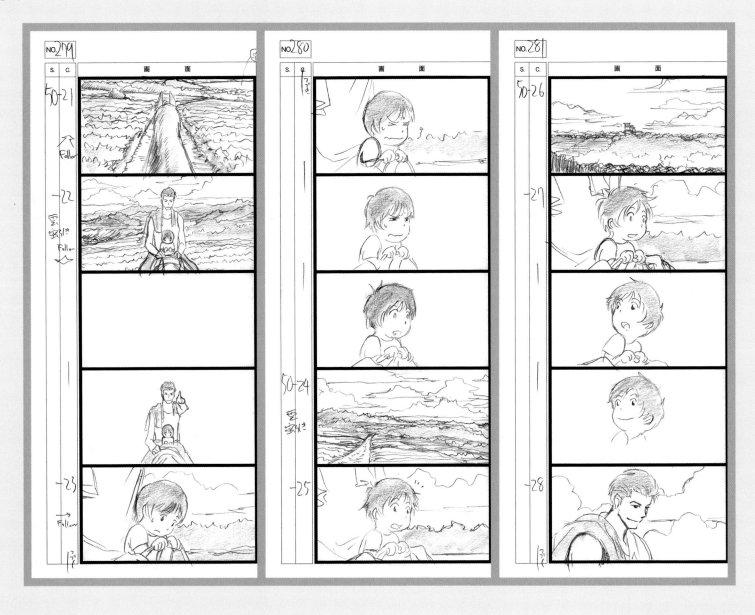

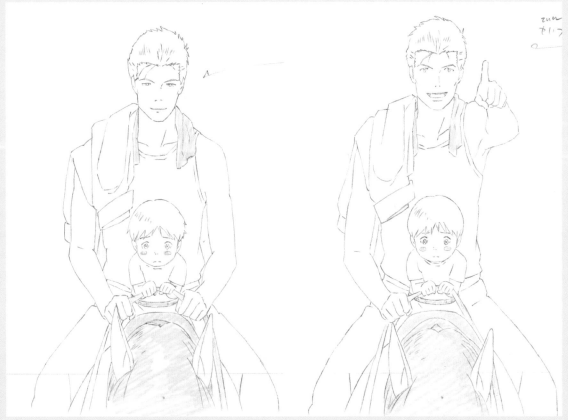

The animation drawings on this spread
show how closely the artists followed
the expressions in the boards.

OPPOSITE, TOP Hosoda's storyboards
of Kun riding with his great-grandfather

OPPOSITE, BOTTOM Kun learns to look
ahead, not down, when he's riding.

THIS PAGE Kun gradually overcomes
his fear and gains confidence.

Kun's most dramatic adventure—and the climax of the film—occurs when he refuses to wear a pair of pants he hates, delaying the family's departure for a vacation. He fusses and hides, then runs to the oak tree. He encounters not another relative, but a sullen teenage version of himself, who dismisses his tantrums. Despite warnings, Kun boards a train that takes him to a huge railway station where he becomes lost and frightened. Hosoda uses a complex mixture of drawn and CG elements to create a menacing world of vast crowds and overscaled arches.

This key sequence posed technical and artistic challenges. Although they call the nightmarish depot "Tokyo Station," the real Tokyo Station is only thirty minutes from Studio Chizu. It felt too familiar to copy literally. The artists instead studied nineteenth-century stations in London and Paris, which felt vast and scary to the designers, just as the fictional Tokyo Station does to Kun.

"The goal was to create something that felt like Tokyo Station despite using distant buildings as models," says production designer Anri Jojo. "I accompanied Hosoda on the scouting trip and was able to experience the stations and dome-like structures firsthand. It helped with the scope and construction of various scenes. Hosoda likes to thoroughly examine any location: In Paris, I racked up twenty-five thousand steps per day."

"Because it is a nightmare, it was a really hard sequence to design. Nothing half-baked or roughly assembled would have worked," Hosoda adds. "We had to exaggerate all the different expressions and emotions. Even using CG models, layering like track upon track of the shinkansen [bullet train] was really difficult. We were trying to depict how we saw the world as children, when everything seemed terrifying and huge."

Kun meets a scornful teenage version of himself, who tells him to get over his tantrum and stop spoiling his family's vacation.

BELOW LEFT **A page of Hosoda's storyboard**

BELOW RIGHT **Frames from the encounter**

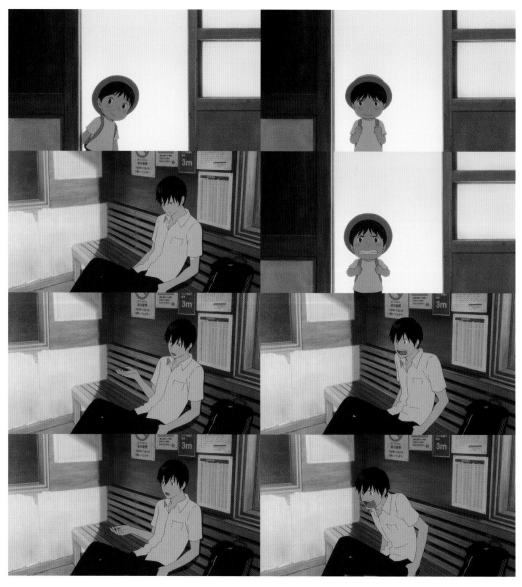

Kun is fascinated by trains,
and these derelict cars
would haunt his nightmares.

After repeatedly being asked to identify himself by a seemingly benevolent robot, the terrified Kun desperately shouts, "I'm Mirai's big brother!" His acceptance of his new place in the family is the correct response: The teenage Mirai arrives to carry him out of the station and back to their house. Passing through an intricate CG web, she explains that the oak tree serves as a nexus, linking all their relatives. When he reenters his home, Kun understands who he is and how he fits into his extended family.

Hosoda points out that the house has "no walls to separate the rooms. It's important we don't have walls, because this is the story of a child learning the family secrets. I wanted him to see -what everyone else was doing. Because it symbolizes what the movie is about, I didn't ask my art director to design the house; I asked an architect. If someone wanted to build that house, they really could."

Small children have always posed a problem for animators. Their short, chubby limbs, slightly awkward proportions, and tentative movements are difficult to capture. They can easily look like hard-edged aliens, miniature adults, or shapeless blobs. As he toddles up and down the many steps in his home, Kun moves with a convincing mixture of energy and uncertainty.

"Japanese animators have mastered the depiction of *kawaii* or cuteness," comments Aoyama. "In real life, a five-year-old kid's head-to-body ratio would be different; we made the head bigger, making him look a little younger. There is a wealth of information and research that's been done in the Japanese animation, which Hosoda encouraged us to draw on and pursue those *kawaii* expressions."

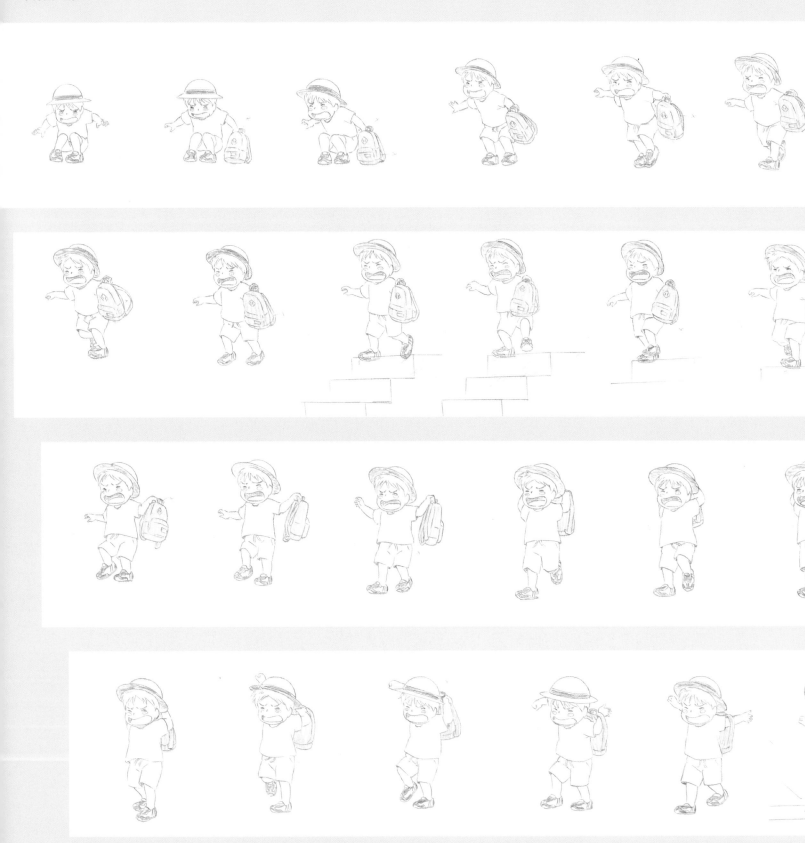

ABOVE Kun cries while shouldering his backpack and walking down the steps to leave home for his fateful trip to Tokyo Station, in these animation drawings. At this point in the film, he's a little older and can handle the stairs more capably.

LEFT Two frames from the scene

TOP **Frustrated by his inability to ride his new bicycle, Kun removes his helmet and hurls it away, in these vivid drawings.**

ABOVE **Two of Hosoda's storyboard drawings**

"To find new ways to portray children in animation, my staff and I observed them firsthand," Hosoda explains. "We invited children to our studio. We played together, we held them, touched their hair. We studied how my son moved and interacted with things. I'm confident that we were successful in animating Kun because we took this extra step—and because the talented animators took on such challenges."

"I have a daughter who's close in age to Hosoda's son; when we were making the movie, they were about Kun's age, so we had a lot of reference material that helped with their exaggerated expressions," adds costume supervisor Daisuke Iga. "We also had a lot of home video we could look at for details, like how kids wear their pants up above their belly buttons."

Kun is not always a likable child. He sulks and fusses and hollers—and his parents react, sometimes in anger, sometimes in confusion. American filmmakers rarely allow their characters to behave disagreeably because they might seem "unlikable." But Kun is more believable than many other animated children because real kids don't behave perfectly.

"In a lot of Western films, not just animated ones, the filmmakers or studios feel compelled to present certain types of characters as perfect. They have no imperfections," says Ralph Eggleston, writer–director of the Oscar-winning Pixar short *For the Birds*. "There's always the phrase that's thrown around, 'That makes the character *unlikable*.' Yes! That's exactly right! *And we have ninety minutes to make them likable again.* Or at least understand them."

Similarly, his parents' efforts to cope with his bad behavior give them an interesting depth and individuality.

"I love the parents because they're not saints. They have regrets and difficulties," Eggleston continues. "They're so believable, so sincere, and so right for that story. There's a lot of high-quality technical expertise put into animated films today, but there aren't many great characters and stories that hold my attention as Hosoda's do."

"It's an extremely realistic portrayal of young adults," agrees Silverman. "The young husband and mother who have interesting, successful lives, and who are trying to balance them with raising two young kids. I can't think of another animated feature that had two adults who are so well fleshed-out: The architect ignores what's going on with his kids, staring at his screen—the creativity is flowing, and he's totally immersed."

"No parents are perfect parents or perfect humans," Hosoda responds. "That's why parents and children need to understand each other and grow together. Perhaps this film is a journey to see the true nature of the people around you—including your parents."

Producer Yuichiro Saito comments, "Hosoda is a director who cares about commercial success, even though he doesn't look at the budget along the way. He understands that commercial success is the ticket to producing the next film. On *Mirai*, I'd almost make the numbers match whatever Hosoda wanted to do—which was tricky. It allowed him a little more freedom in his choices. People in the industry accused me of spoiling him."

Mirai also earned rave reviews (scoring 90 percent Fresh on Rotten Tomatoes). In the *New York Times*, Bilge Ebiri wrote, "Hosoda's film privileges moments of emotion over belabored story mechanics. Thus, it gathers complexity without sacrificing any of its guileless modesty. In the best possible way, *Mirai* feels like the dream of a very wise child." The *Daily Telegraph*'s Robbie Collin said, "Great animation can put its finger on the essence of a human feeling or experience like that, often with a precision and insight that even the best live-action performances can't match—and *Mirai* bathes ordinary family life in a beautiful new light."

RIGHT Kun throws a tantrum. Although real children have fits, very few American animated kids do.

OPPOSITE Hosoda's storyboard shows Kun's tantrum upsetting the baby, his mother, and even the dog.

NO. 56 スタジオ 地図

S.C.	画面	内容	TIME	MUSIC	EFFECT

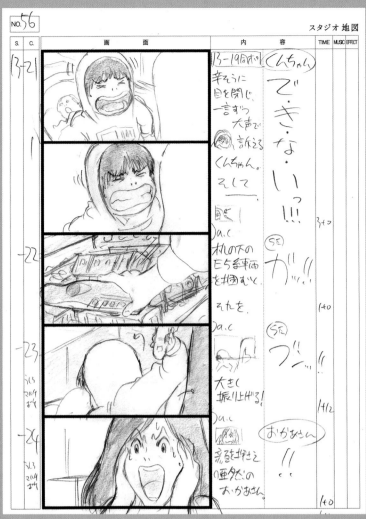

13-21
13-19のオドリ
辛そうに目を閉じ一言ずつ大声で訴えるくんちゃん。そして—

(くんちゃん)
で・き・な・い！！

-22
机の下のE5系車両を掴むく それを

SE
が・・・！！

-23
大きく振り上げる！

SE
ブン・・・！！

-24
親を捨てる亜夕のおかあさん。

(おかあさん)
！！

NO. 58 スタジオ 地図

S.C.	画面	内容	TIME	MUSIC	EFFECT

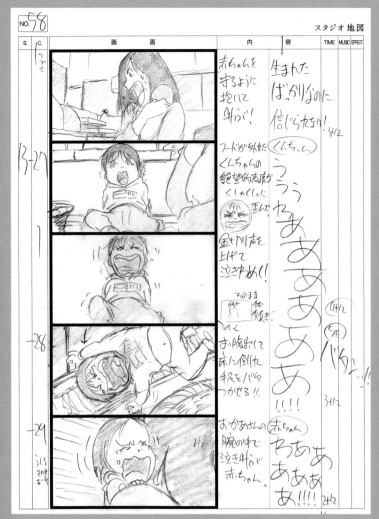

13-27
赤ちゃんを守るように抱いて叫ぶが！

生まれたばかりなのに信じられない！

フードが外れたくんちゃんの絶望的な表情がくしゃくしゃに

(くんちゃん)
うう

-28
金切り声を上げて泣き叫ぶ！！
そのまま体傾き
お腹おさえて床に倒れ足をバタつかせる！！

あああ
ああ
ああ
！！！！
(SE)
バタン・・・！！

-29
おかあさんの腕の中で泣き叫ぶ赤ちゃん

(赤ちゃん)
ちあああああ
あ！！！！

NO. 57 スタジオ 地図

S.C.	画面	内容	TIME	MUSIC	EFFECT

13-25
13-7同ポ
E5系で赤ちゃんの頭を叩くくんちゃんの手。

SE
ガツッ・・・！！

何が先こったか分からないほど茫然とした赤ちゃん。みるみる涙があふれ火が点いたように激しく泣き叫ぶ！！

(赤ちゃん)
ああああ
あああ
ああ
あ

-26
おかあさん赤ちゃんに見とれているように見えない！勢いでくんちゃん倒される。

(おかあさん)
なにすんの

(くんちゃん)
あ・・！！

NO. 59 スタジオ 地図

S.C.	画面	内容	TIME	MUSIC	EFFECT

13-30
わっこもかって来て遊びにする！

(わっこ)
わっこちゃん
おて
おて
ん！

-31
その光景を茫然と見てはおとうさん。

(おとうさん)
・・・・・・！！

-32
おかあさん、恐い顔で振り返り。赤ちゃんをおとうさんに渡すと

(おかあさん)
見とまって
ちょっと！

(おとうさん)
あー
はいはい

195

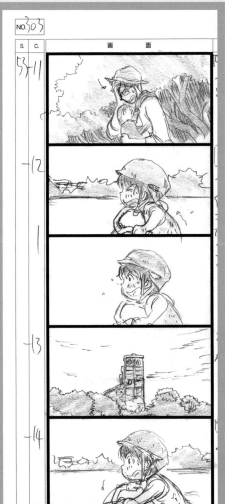

After his great-grandfather's explanation, Kun succeeds
in riding his bike.

OPPOSITE, LEFT **Hosoda's storyboards of the scene**

OPPOSITE, TOP RIGHT AND MIDDLE **Two animation
drawings**

OPPOSITE, BOTTOM MIDDLE AND RIGHT **Two stills**

FAR LEFT **Additional storyboards**

ABOVE AND LEFT **Kun's father cheers his son's success,
in animation drawings and a frame from the film.**

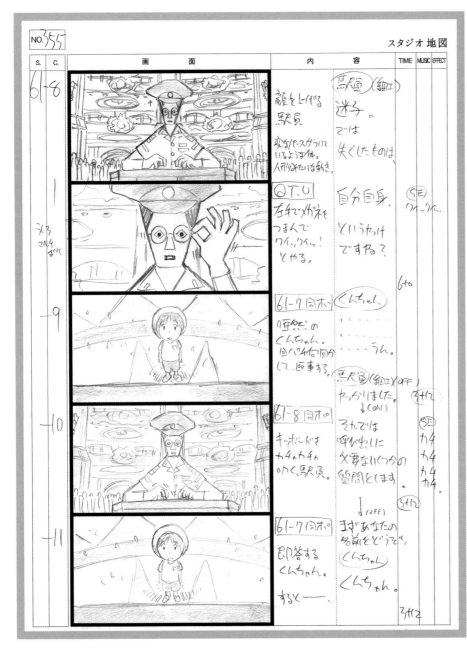

Kun seeks help from Lost & Found Man, but he is unable to supply the requested information.

TOP Hosoda's storyboards of the frustrating exchange

ABOVE AND RIGHT Frames of the scene

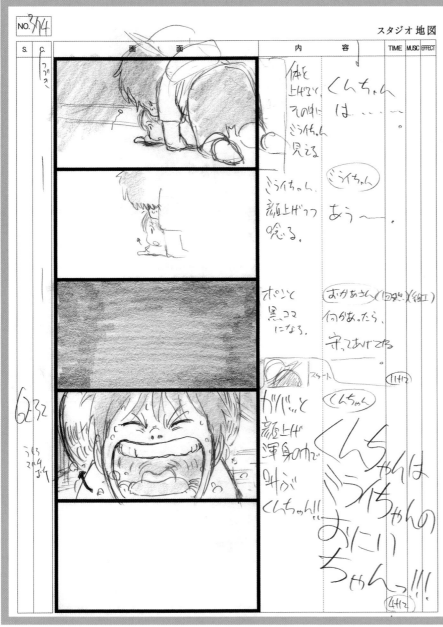

At the climax of the film, Kun prevents Mirai from boarding a threatening train and discovers the correct answer to the Lost & Found Man's repeated question, "Who are you?" "I'm Mirai's big brother!"

TOP Hosoda's storyboards of Kun's declaration

ABOVE AND RIGHT Frames of the scene

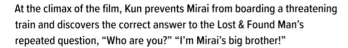

Kun's acceptance of his new place in the family breaks the spell. The older Mirai carries him away from the sinister station, through the web that links him to his family members past and present, and back to his home.

RIGHT Panels from Hosoda's storyboards

OPPOSITE, LEFT Frames from the sequence

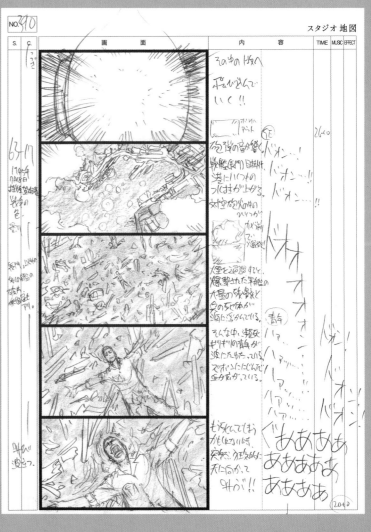

Hosoda won a fifth Japanese Academy Award for Animation of the Year for *Mirai*. Outside Japan, the film premiered at the Directors' Fortnight, which runs parallel to the Cannes Film Festival. *Mirai* became the first Japanese film not produced by Studio Ghibli to be nominated for the Academy Award for Best Animated Feature. It was also the first Japanese film nominated for a Golden Globe for animated feature. It won the Annie Award for Best Independent Animated Feature.

"The awards and recognition have some relevance when we are opening conversations about different financial models—or the motivation to make something together in the future," says Saito. "They carry a lot of meaning."

The success of *Mirai* confirms what other award-winning animation directors from Hayao Miyazaki to Tomm Moore have shown: If an artist tells a story about his family or culture honestly and well, it becomes universal.

"This movie is about a family that lives in a small corner of Japan, but when we show it worldwide, people think of it as their own story," Hosoda concludes. "They feel the things the Japanese audience feels. Showing your movies is like trying to make friends with the audience. I feel I've made friends with different people in different parts of the world with *Mirai*."

ABOVE Hosoda and producer Yuichiro Saito pose at the Oscar nominees luncheon.

HOUSE DESIGN

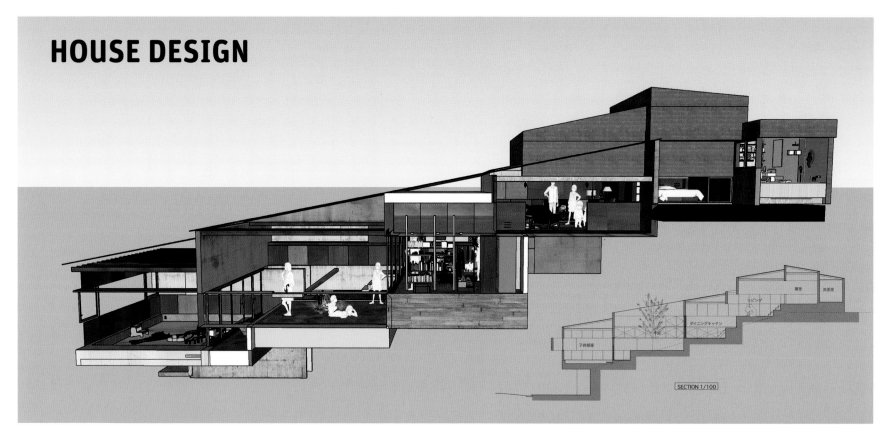

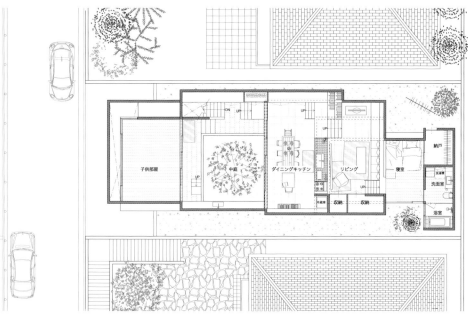

Various architectural renderings of Kun's family home. Drawings of the figures suggest the scale of the rooms. Hosoda says, "If someone wanted to build that house, they really could."

Two detailed background paintings
of the dining room

NIGHTMARE TRAINS

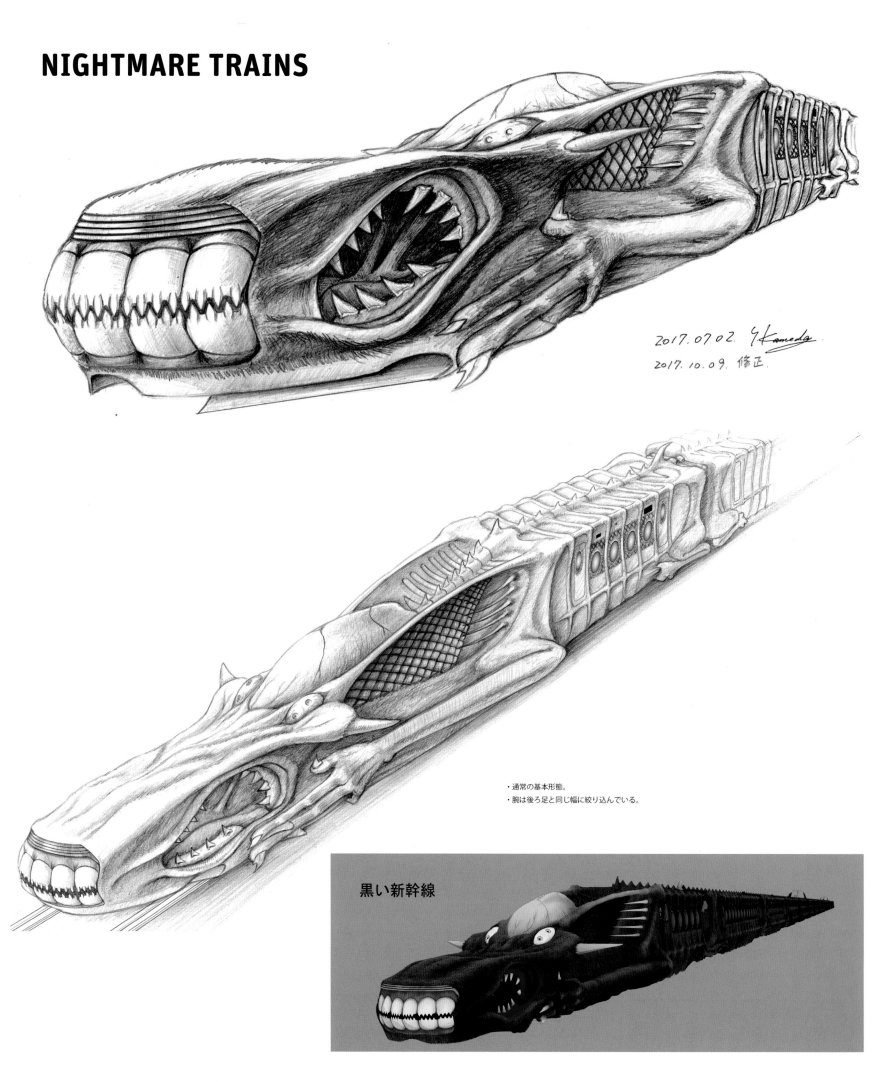

2017.07.02. Y.Kameda.
2017.10.09. 修正.

・通常の基本形態。
・腕は後ろ足と同じ幅に絞り込んでいる。

黒い新幹線

OPPOSITE **Original designs for the black bullet train that resembles a vicious monster, by Kameda Yoshitaka, who worked at Kawasaki Heavy Indsutries, Ltd., on the Shinkansen "bullet trains" Kun adores.**

THIS PAGE **The final CG version of the train; the sinister exterior pales before the skeletal seats. Kun's jealousy is eclipsed by the need to save his sister from this terrible conveyance.**

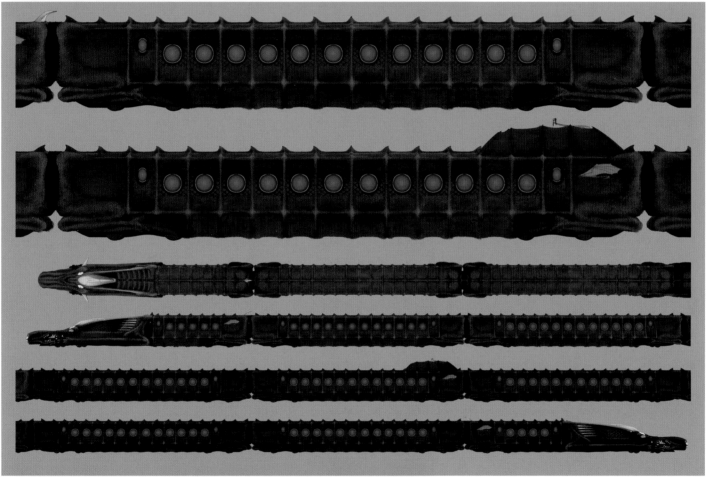

TOKYO STATION

ABOVE A preliminary study for the fictional Tokyo Station reflects the nineteenth-century European buildings Hosoda and his crew studied.

LEFT An early visualization of the Lost & Found Man at his kiosk

OPPOSITE Background studies

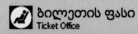

The familiar signage in Tokyo Station make its overscaled spaces feel even more threatening.

BOTTOM RIGHT A preliminary study of the main hall

The great wrought-iron beams and stone arches in the central rotunda of the station make the setting more intimidating to Kun—and the audience.

LOST & FOUND MAN

Preliminary sketches of the Lost & Found Man and Clockman. Comments include the note that Clockman is modeled on the pocket watches carried by the train station staff.

OPPOSITE Stages in creating the CG version of the final character

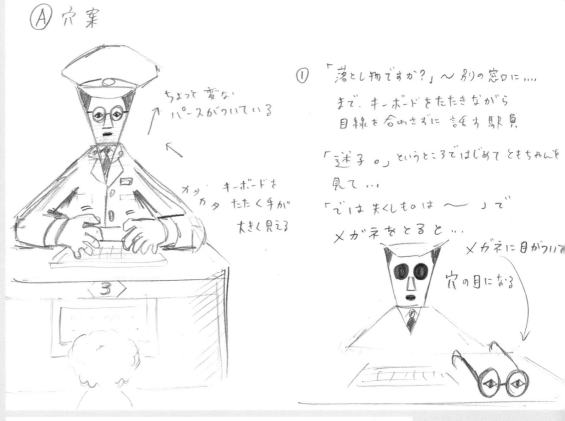

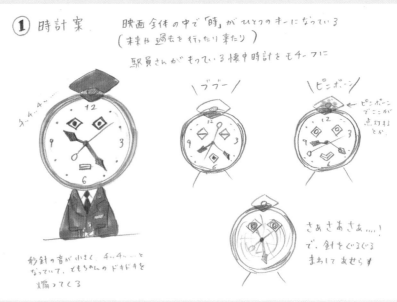

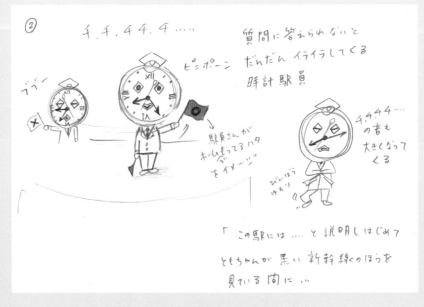

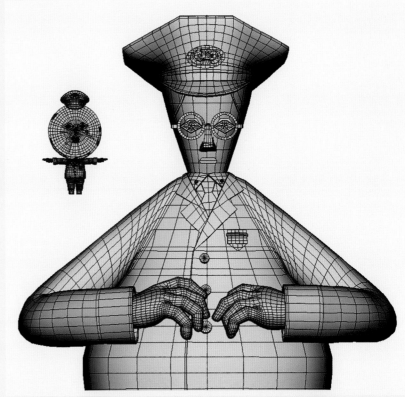

口閉じ

目閉じ・おちょぼ口

Secure in his new identity, Kun
gets along with his sister and
even makes her laugh.

OPPOSITE Hosoda's storyboard
of the final scene

ABOVE Two frames of the children
sharing a laugh

未来のミライ

未来のミライ

ボクは未来に出会った。

小さな庭から時をこえる旅へ——
それは、ボクと家族の未来をめぐる物語。

上白石萌歌　黒木 華
星野 源　麻生久美子　吉原光夫　宮崎美子
役所広司

監督・脚本・原作：細田 守
作画監督：青山浩行　秦 綾子　美術監督：大森 崇　髙松洋平　音楽：髙木正勝　オープニングテーマ・主題歌：山下達郎
D.N.ドリームパートナーズ・スタジオ地図LLP 共同事業
NTTドコモ　日本テレビ放送網　KADOKAWA　スタジオ地図
プロモーションパートナーズ
東宝　読売テレビ放送　バップ　電通
BTV　MMT　SDT　CTV　HTV　FBS　ローソン　シェイクアール東日本企画　ワーナーミュージック・ジャパン　LINE　読売新聞社
企画・制作：スタジオ地図
ゼネラルプロデューサー：奥田 誠　プロデューサー：齋藤優一郎　伊藤卓哉　逆立誠一　山村元気　ラインプロデューサー：平田大樹　アソシエイトプロデューサー：伊藤 整　横山 慶　町田有也　笠原可江
画面設計：山下高明　美術設計：三辻 修　CGディレクター：電影研　友美　企画協力：伊藤卓大　プロダクションデザイン：上條安里　佐伯 誠　tupera tupera　亀田光来　小野委夫
編集：西山 茂　洋楽・企画技術：有村修古　音響効果：柴田康至　録音プロデューサー：森幸長　キャスティングディレクター：溝田絹加　今西美子

7.20
[FRI] ROADSHOW
@未来のミライ mirai-no-mirai.jp

『時をかける少女』『サマーウォーズ』
『おおかみこどもの雨と雪』
『バケモノの子』

細田 守監督最新作

MARKETING

Licensed products included a plush version of the tail Kun steals from Yukko, mugs and glasses, a jar of marshmallows, and a stuffed Yukko.

OPPOSITE **The poster for** *Mirai*

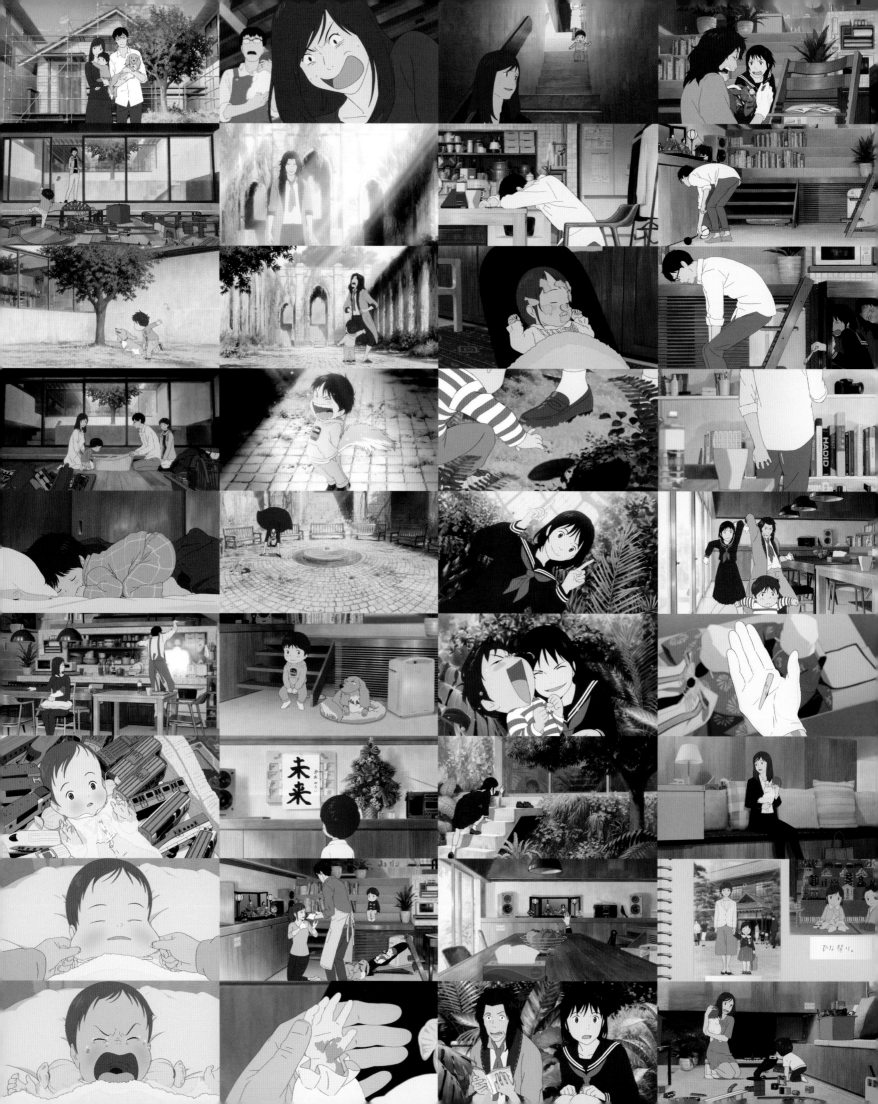

竜とそばかすの姫

VII. BELLE

Belle is the movie that I have always wanted to create, and I am only able to make this film a reality because of the culmination of my past work. I explore romance, action, and suspense on the one hand, and deeper themes, such as life and death, on the other.

—MAMORU HOSODA

Mirai brought Mamoru Hosoda unprecedented inter-

national attention. Japanese audiences, Western anime fans, and animators who follow the festival circuit already knew his work. But the screening at Cannes and the Oscar nomination attracted wider audiences, bringing him recognition as one of the most interesting directors working in animation.

"With *Mirai*, we traveled to the United States, which had seemed like such a distant world to me," he says. "Words like 'Oscar' and 'Golden Globe' hadn't really resonated with me: They felt like distant things that happened somewhere on the other side of the planet. The response to *Mirai* widened my perspective. I realized it was possible to make a movie that can be viewed and enjoyed around the world."

For his next film, Hosoda chose a story he had been thinking about for many years: *Beauty and the Beast*. The fairy tale had already been filmed at least thirty times, beginning with the 1899 French live-action version by Pathé Frères. But the best known films are Jean Cocteau's surreal black-and-white *La Belle et la Bête* (1946) and the hugely popular 1991 Disney musical.

"I researched many different interpretations and adaptations of *Beauty and the Beast* for this production, but the Disney and Cocteau versions are the pillars for me," Hosoda says. "*Beauty and the Beast* has been interpreted and reinterpreted so many times throughout the years; that tells me the story presents some very human truths. But it needs to be transformed and updated to fit the needs of modern society.

"Making the heroine in Disney's *Beauty and the Beast* a contemporary young woman represented a major shift," he continues. "When you think of animation and female leads, you always go to the fairy-tale tropes. But they really broke that template: It felt very new. Similarly, what we're trying to do in *Belle* is not build a character, but build a person. We're creating someone who reflects the society in which we live. That's what gives new projects meaning to me."

PREVIOUS SPREAD **A classic meeting reimagined: The avatars of Belle and the Dragon meet in his castle in the cyber world of U.**

OPPOSITE **A preliminary study of Belle in costume. Artist: Jin Kim**

BELOW **Hosoda found the inspiration in two classic films of the Beauty and the Beast legend: Jean Cocteau's stylized *La Belle et la Bête* (1946) and Disney's animated musical (1991).**

鈴 SUZU

OPPOSITE **The model sheets of Suzu emphasize her appearance as a normal girl from a small town, completely removed from the glamour Belle embodies.**

ABOVE **Suzu's room feels like it belongs to an everyday girl in high school.**

Suzu resembles neither Cocteau's proud, mature Belle, nor the independent intellectual in the Disney film—nor the passive merchant's daughter of the traditional fairy tale. She is not beautiful or sought-after. Suzu is a withdrawn, lonely teenager, living with her father in a small town in Shikoku. She's still dealing with the loss of her mother, who drowned rescuing a little girl from the nearby river. She misses her mother, but is angry that her parent abandoned her to "rescue a kid whose name she didn't even know."

"When we were developing Suzu, she was supposed to be an introvert, not someone who stood out," says animation director Hiroyuki Aoyama. "We tried extending her bangs, perhaps hiding her eyes—very visually introverted. We added freckles, skewing her away from a traditional 'cute' character. A lot of her animated performance was already in the storyboards. Hosoda's storyboards carry so much information, down to the character's expressions. As animators, we just followed them."

"Suzu has a lot of suppressed feelings," adds Hosoda. "There are a lot of things she wants to do but can't. She's a character who looks down at the ground as she walks down the street. She's very far from what I would call a 'free' character."

Despite her withdrawn nature, Suzu has friends. Her childhood companion Shinobu has kept his promise to protect her since her mother died. Over the years, he's grown into a tall, athletic young man. Hiro, her energetic best friend, tries to push Suzu out of her shell—and stage-manages Suzu's appearances as Belle in the cyber world of U. Good-humored Kamishin constantly tries—without success—to recruit students (especially girls) for his kayak club. Suzu is surprised when Luka, the class leader with a model's good looks, reaches out to her.

Suzu's mother had encouraged her early interest in music. The trauma of her death left Suzu unable to display her musical talent in front of anyone. She seems like the last person whose alter ego would be the reigning diva of the cyber realm. Yet Belle is beloved by countless fans around the world. As her big production numbers demonstrate, her music touches their hearts while her performance dazzles their eyes. Tall, assured, and fantastically costumed (including a dress made of living flowers), Belle is the embodiment of glamour.

Although Hosoda had combined drawn animation and CG in his previous films with exceptional skill, the computer animation had been restricted to background elements and effects, including the whale in *The Boy and the Beast*. *Belle* incorporates CG animation of the principal characters in their U-forms.

Hosoda asked Jin Kim, a South Korean artist who had worked on *Frozen*, *Moana*, and other contemporary Disney films, to design the CG Belle. "I'm a huge fan of Hosoda's movies; he understands teenage emotions and portrays them so perfectly," says Kim. "When I read the script, I was struck by how his approach was so fresh and different. And the subject he's dealing with is so heavy. It's hard to imagine this kind of story in American animation."

Athletic, overly enthusiastic Kamishin and Luka, the most popular girl in the school, discover their mutual attraction—with a little help from Suzu. The moment captures the awkward vulnerability of teenage romances and provides comic relief for the more serious main story.

LEFT AND OPPOSITE, FAR RIGHT **Sensitive** animation drawings by Takayuki Hamada

ベル BELLE

As befits the reigning diva of U, Belle's costumes and accessories are extravagant, even over the top. Only a superstar performer could pull them off. Artist: Takaaki Yamashita

BOTTOM RIGHT Animator Takaaki Yamashita (shooting reference footage of a fountain) says, "We skewed Suzu away from what a traditional cute character would be. As for animating her and creating the performance, a lot of that was in the storyboards. Hosoda's storyboards are just excellent in terms of how much expression they carry, how much information he's able to put into them."

コート姿

226

For inspiration, Kim studied a number of divas, including Lady Gaga, Beyoncé, K-Pop stars, and the South Korean coloratura soprano Sumi Jo. He adds, "Many of my drawings were based on poses and attitudes Sumi Jo adopts when she sings."

To create the CG animation, Hosoda once again turned to Ryo Horibe and Digital Frontier, who had worked on his previous films. One of the biggest challenges Horibe and his artists faced was the production number of Belle's hit song. Dances are notoriously difficult to animate: The movements are complicated, they overlap, and the individual steps must match the beats of the music. For *Snow White and the Seven Dwarfs* (1937), Walt Disney's animators worked from live-action footage of dancer Marge Champion; Horibe's artists used the modern equivalent, motion capture, to analyze the motions.

"We brought the dancer who choreographed the song to our mo-cap [motion-capture] stage to give us the basic movements, which we adjusted by hand," Horibe explains. "We knew singing would be an important element before we got into animation, so we looked at some Western artists, including Ariana Grande. But for the actual animation, we didn't reference anyone but the dancer. Belle also has a lot of scenes in the movie in which she's not singing: There's day-to-day interactions with the other characters, including some dramatic moments, all of which we did without mo-cap reference."

TOP AND ABOVE Belle's facial patterning suggests a combination of makeup and sixties body-painting.

LEFT The folds of fabric in Belle's scarlet dress echo the curving petals of a dahlia.

BELOW CG Animator/director Ryo Horibe comments, "For both Belle and the Dragon, we were trying to express how you can feel very lonely within this massive metropolis. We used all the tools we had our disposal to bring that emotion forward and create the performances the director was looking for."

Character designer Jin Kim's development drawings are so vivid, they seem to have already been animated. Kim (RIGHT) explains, "When you design a character, it's not just designing a face or a body shape: The costume is a big part of the design—and a big part of the character. I wanted to keep Belle not too modern, but not too classical; something timeless. It was challenging to keep that fine line."

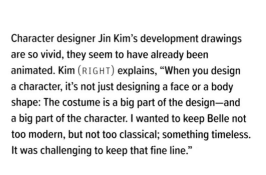

OPPOSITE Belle pauses on the castle stairs, in this preliminary drawing.

THIS PAGE Three studies of Belle swathed in a cape that opens to reveal another striking gown. Artist: Jin Kim

If animating the lead characters in CG required the artists to stretch their talents, it also forced Hosoda to alter his approach to directing. "He had to adapt how he directed the artists," Horibe says. "When we're working with hand-drawn images, he would draw on top of the animators' work to readjust a pose or expression. In CG, a lot of the feedback had to come through words. He would watch a sequence with the animator and verbally explain the adjustments he wanted."

In Cocteau's film, Josette Day says, "The beast suffers....His eyes are so sad"; Disney's Belle discovers loneliness and generosity beneath Beast's gruff façade. The beast Suzu encounters—referred to as "the Dragon"—is not a prince seeking to break a sorceress's spell, but a boy who has been abused by his father. Unable to protect his younger brother, Tomo, from their father's wrath, Kei created an avatar who can fight off any enemy he faces. With his long jaws, fangs, and powerful limbs, the Dragon is a formidable foe. But his tattered cloak, sagging shoulders, and drooping head reflect Kei's wounded psyche.

Child abuse is a subject rarely, if ever, mentioned in Western animated films. But as the father of two young children, Hosoda felt he needed to address the issue: "If you don't include these themes in your movies, it's the equivalent of averting your eyes from a problem. Back in the day, it was completely normal to smack your kids if they misbehaved. Now we all agree that's a bad thing. Just because society has shifted to that mindset doesn't mean the problem has disappeared.

"You want your kids to live in an absolute dream world, but that's not always the case: That reality needs to be reflected in the projects we make," he continues. "We could simply make a genre film that follows a template and provides some entertainment—and that's OK. But I feel creators, in whatever medium, have almost an obligation to bring these messages to people's attention. We can't

ignore what's going on. Maybe the theme is a little shocking, but is it shocking to depict reality in an animated film?"

The first time the audience sees the Dragon, he fights off the vigilante Justin and the self-proclaimed guardians of order in U. His complex, part-human/part-animal anatomy made him a challenge to animate.

"The Dragon has a very elongated face, and his body is quite large. It's very hard to animate that type of creature," Horibe explains. "We were inspired by what Glen Keane did in the Disney film; we tried to keep the aura or feel his Beast had. When the Dragon first appears, he's fighting. There's a lot of *Dragon Ball*–esque action moves you wouldn't associate with an animal as much as with the hero of an anime series or a manga. We didn't want the animal elements in his design to be too restricting of his movements."

The Dragon initially seems like a villain, but as the story unfolds, the audience develops a sympathy for his plight. The animators had to suggest the sorrow and pain that underlay his aggressive behavior.

"For the most part, we followed what Hosoda had drawn in the storyboards, which is how we got some of those subtle nuances," Horibe continues. "The sum of the details on the screen, like the Dragon's standing pose and sharp eyes, somehow gives off the vibe that he's lonely. We worked to achieve that emotion."

British architect and designer Eric Wong was chosen to create the look of the cyber-world U. "Digital Frontier

スタジオ地図

S.C.	画面	内容	TIME	MUSIC	EFFECT

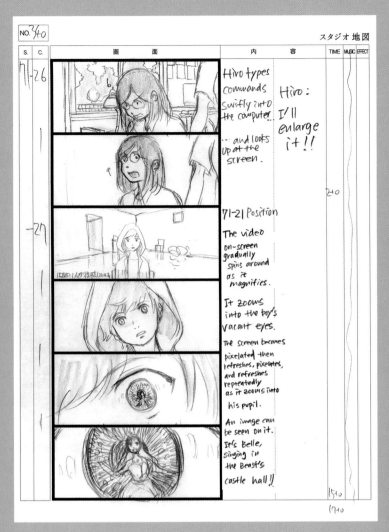

71-26

Hiro types commands swiftly into the computer... and looks up at the screen.

Hiro: I'll enlarge it!!

-27 / 71-21 Position

The video on-screen gradually spins around as it magnifies.

It zooms into the boy's vacant eyes.

The screen becomes pixelated then refreshes, pixelates, and refreshes repeatedly as it zooms into his pupil.

An image can be seen on it. It's Belle, singing in the Beast's castle hall!!

17+0

スタジオ地図

71-31

Hiro gasps at the sudden loud noise coming from the monitor.

SE (on-screen): BANG!!
Hiro: Huh?! (+0)
SE (on-screen): SLAM!!

-32

Suzu gasps at the next noise.

Suzu: ...! (14+2)

-33 / 71-21 Position

A man, seemingly his father, walks in slowly from the hallway.

He stands tall and straight with his chest out.

His voice is quiet, patient.

However, Tomo doesn't respond and just stands there rocking back and forth.

Then suddenly, the father strikes out and knocks over the flower vase. It clatters onto floor!!

e.g. Tomo slowly falls onto his bottom.

Father (on-screen): (humming stops)
Tomo: What's with that song?
Tomo (on-screen):
Father (on-screen): You know I'm working. Don't you think it's a little distracting?
Tomo (on-screen): ...
SE (on-screen): CRASH!! (22+0)

24+12

スタジオ地図

71-28 / Position

Suzu is stunned.

The image of the boy is projected onto Suzu's eyes.

Suzu: ... It's Belle. ... (4+0)

-29 / 71-21 Position

The boy continues humming as he stands up and then goes to the back of the room with a jaunty stride.

Something about the boy seems off.

The room has one entrance and a single window. On the wall is wallpaper with flying birds printed on it. There's a red rose in a vase.

Hiro (OFF): So, is he the Beast?
Suzu (OFF): But, something's weird... (9+0)

-30 / 69-4 Position

The two stare at the monitor. Suzu looks at Hiro. Hiro also makes eye contact with Suzu. Then--

Hiro: What do you mean "weird"?
Suzu: I just can't believe that this boy is him.
Hiro: You're right. It doesn't look like he has any scars... (14+0)

20+0

スタジオ地図

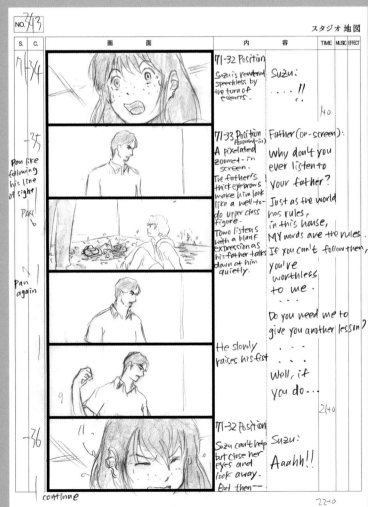

71-34 / Position

Suzu is rendered speechless by the turn of events.

Suzu: ...!! (+0)

-35 / 71-33 Position (zoomed-in)

A pixelated zoomed-in screen. The father's thick eyebrows make him look like a well-to-do upper class figure. Tomo listens with a blank expression as his father talks down at him quietly.

Pan like following his line of sight. PAN

Pan again

He slowly raises his fist.

Father (on-screen): Why don't you ever listen to your father? Just as the world has rules, in this house, MY words are the rules. If you can't follow them, you're worthless to me. Do you need me to give you another lesson? ... Well, if you do... (2+0)

-36 / 71-32 Position

Suzu can't help but close her eyes and look away. But then--

Suzu: Aaahh!!

continue

22+0

233

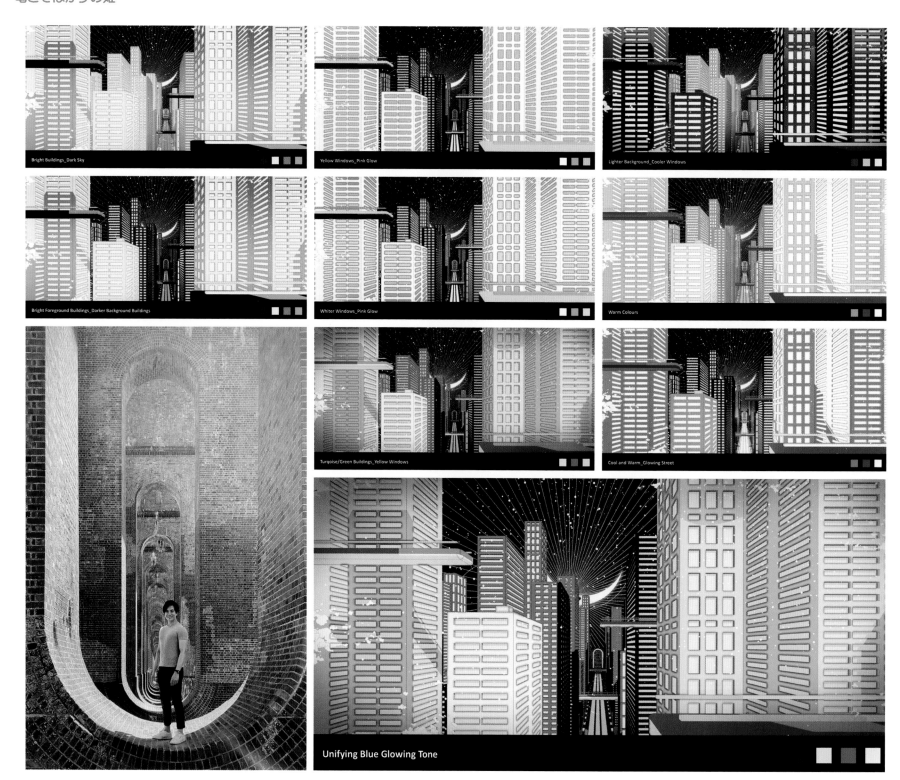

Bright Buildings_Dark Sky

Yellow Windows_Pink Glow

Lighter Background_Cooler Windows

Bright Foreground Buildings_Darker Background Buildings

Whiter Windows_Pink Glow

Warm Colours

Turqoise/Green Buildings_Yellow Windows

Cool and Warm_Glowing Street

Unifying Blue Glowing Tone

ABOVE AND OPPOSITE **Designer/architect Eric Wong** experimented with various palettes for the perpetually twilit realm of U. Some of the color schemes were derived from sunsets, neon, and aurora borealis. Wong (standing on the Ouse Valley Viaduct) recalls, "Working on *Belle* was an amazing experience. I'd send Studio Chizu a pack of artwork almost every week. I'd have to get up super early in the morning because of the time difference, and then go to work, then come home to work on *Belle* in the evenings and on weekends. It was tough, but it was exciting because Hosoda gave me a lot of freedom to pursue the design of the city."

contacted me one day to do some concept art for them, but they didn't tell me who or what film it was for. They just gave me three or four sentences," he recalls. "I sent them a concept pack based on those few words. After that, they told me, 'You'll be working with director Hosoda and his team at Studio Chizu.' I loved Hosoda's work when I was growing up: I remember watching *Digimon* as a kid, then seeing all of his films as an adult."

Wong's initial designs played off the signature U-shape. "I imagined something based on various references and architectural typologies of castles. It was this U-shaped castle with typical walls and gates and courtyards and moats," he explains. "Hosoda said, 'I liked the work, but can you do a version that's reminiscent of *Summer Wars*?' So I revisited the city as if it were *OZ* 2.0. There was a crown, orbiting features, castles, speakers, skyscrapers, transport portals, a giant whale, and a moon."

But Hosoda changed his mind and told Wong to go back to his original ideas, which were more intricate and rectilinear. Because Hosoda wanted a nocturnal atmosphere for U,

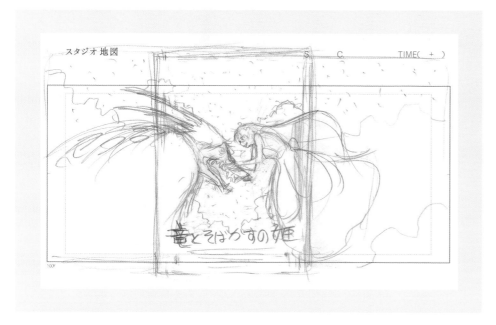

ABOVE Hosoda's pencil sketch for publicity art for Belle

RIGHT The final image. This touching portrait of the main characters appeared in numerous formats, including the cover of the souvenir booklet published by Toho for the film's opening.

Wong experimented with palettes adapted from evening skies around the world, and altered the scale of the signature crescent moon. This new version felt colder and infinitely larger: U went from being a world that could be captured in one view to a mega-structure that seems to go on forever.

Wong's vision of U suggests a cross between a metropolis and a motherboard: complex, intricately detailed, and orderly. If Manhattan or Tokyo were somehow exponentially enlarged, the resulting city would resemble U. Serried ranks of buildings continue to infinity in every direction. The opening sequence, which leads the viewer into U, dazzles the eye with its complexity. U feels like a place of unlimited opportunity—and the embodiment of urban alienation. The animators at Digital Frontier had to create performances that could hold the viewer's attention, despite the distraction of the complex setting.

"Belle and the Dragon express how you can feel very lonely within these massive metropolitan visuals," adds Horibe. "A few times, the director said, 'I want it to feel like the whole screen is being engulfed by these buildings.' Even among those myriad buildings, we used all of the tools that we had at our disposal to bring the emotion and performance of the characters forward."

In *Summer Wars*, the bright colors and rounded shapes of OZ feel warm, inviting, and even childish. Although it's vast, OZ appears navigable and welcoming: Outside of the designated battle areas, visitors know they're safe. In contrast, U suggests an unknown city seen from a hotel window: precise, angular, vast, and aloof. Hosoda chose this colder world to reflect changes in the ways people use the

Internet, which has become a staging ground for culture wars, disinformation campaigns, and personal vendettas.

"When *Summer Wars* was first released, there were a lot of comparisons to *Digimon*: 'We're entering this cyber world—ah, it's the same movie,'" Hosoda states. "But they're completely different environments and different movies. *Digimon* came out in 2000; *Summer Wars* was 2009. There had been a massive shift in how we used the Internet and how the Internet had affected our lives. The Internet really began exploding in the 2000s; it seemed like a place of hope, where the younger generation would drive the path forward. That was an overarching theme in *Digimon*, where the younger generation had to rise to the challenge.

"Fast forward to 2009—and today—and no one really sees the Internet that way anymore," he continues. "Over the last twenty years, we've gotten more tools, including

social media. A lot of people are on the Internet to harm others under a veil of anonymity, which shows how the Internet has shifted. But I believe there are going to be new ways to use the Internet for better causes. I want to push that message: In spite of everything, kids will pave a path to a new world. That idea led to *Belle*. There are people who use the Internet in different ways in the film, but the underlying theme is hope."

In contrast to metropolitan complexities of U, Hosoda set the "real world" elements of *Belle* in the Kochi Prefecture of southern Shikoku. Like the mountainous setting in *Wolf Children*, rural Kochi is facing depopulation as younger people move to cities. The bus Suzu rides to school has a sign warning that the service will be discontinued in September.

"The kind of pressures Suzu feels had to be depicted in her immediate surroundings," Hosoda explains. "When you

immerse yourself in the deep rural areas, you get the sense they're on the brink of destruction. It feels like the edge of the world. The art director and I talked a lot about how to capture that feeling in the movie."

The COVID-19 pandemic prevented Hosoda and his crew from taking their usual scouting trips. "We were in lockdown, so we reached out to the film commission of the territory and did a kind of remote scouting," Hosoda says. "The film commissioner would go around holding up a camera and we'd say, 'Can you stop there? Can you zoom in on that?' When you scout locations, you breathe in the air and feel different vibes than you get from a photograph. But thinking about this project's themes taking place in the Internet, having the scouting done remotely seems both ironic and appropriate."

Art director Nobutaka Ike's father was from Kochi, which gave the setting a personal resonance. Although he agrees the commissioner captured many useful details, art directors have special ways of looking at scenery.

"Whether it's the side of a road or a telephone pole, there are certain elements only an art director would think to look at or zoom in on. It was hard to get the film commission members to point the camera in those directions," Ike sighs. "For me, this story is about Suzu recapturing a part of herself that she's lost. For most of the story she's trying to fight off this negativity. We use the beauty of Kochi as a brighter side."

The setting for *Belle* also reflects a recurring theme in Hosoda's work: the changing seasons in Japan. Ike notes that phenomenon cannot be defined or explained logically; the film reflects Hosoda's vision of the seasons in Kochi. Suzu often walks along the banks of the Niyodo River, and her trips at different times of the year both parallel and contrast with her journeys through the rectilinear, urban U.

"The idea of four seasons and transitioning between them is a fundamental of Japanese aesthetics," Hosoda says. "People live in seasons, and this idea permeates all of my films. I'm interested in the idea of change; people who don't change are boring. The seasons are a good way to tie that all together."

Hosoda extended the seasonal imagery to U, as Wong recalls, "He really enjoyed the look of the linear city. He said, 'It's also like a river, isn't it? Like a river flowing, much like the scenes in the real world where Suzu walks past the river.' So, it had this poetic resonance. It was a combination of all of the metaphors that solidified into this almost string-like city."

The storyboard specifies, "Suzu's house stands on a hill in a village deep in the mountains." In keeping with his belief that a home in an animated film tells the audience important details about a character, Hosoda describes it as "a house that isn't very traditional or very new. It had to be in the middle: the kind of house you would see on the outskirts of town collecting a little dust." Surrounded by trees and greenery, Suzu's home suggests a pleasant but fading community—a town families move away from, but families rarely move to.

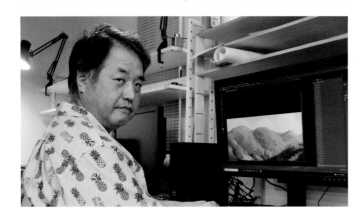

LEFT Art director Nobutaka Ike explains, "For me, this story is about Suzu recapturing a part of herself that she's lost. She's going through this very negative atmosphere and trying to fight off that negativity. Yet Kochi is very beautiful. We focused on Kochi and how the sunlight illuminates a lot of the environment—the brighter side."

BELOW Nozu Elementary School in Kochi Prefecture in Shikoku served as a partial model for the school in the film. The notes on the floor plan and aerial view indicate where the main facilities and key rooms are located.

Nozu elementary school

〈能津小学校（廃校小学校モデル）見取り図〉

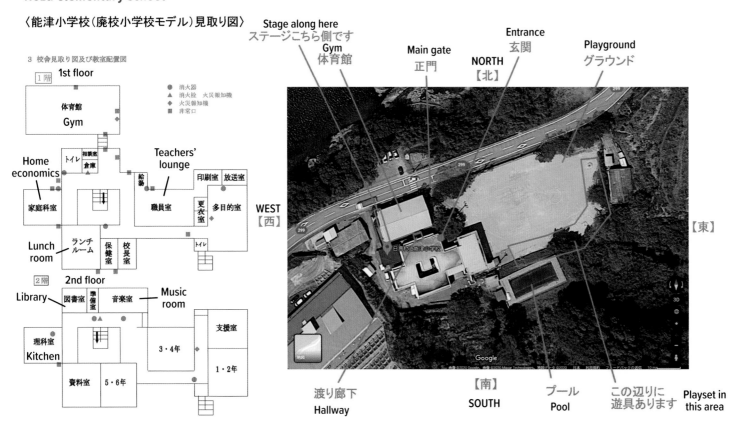

スタジオ 地図   S.   C.   TIME(+   )

AM 10:00

ABOVE LEFT **A layout drawing of one building**

LEFT **The fully rendered background**

"Suzu's environment was her room, and it was thought out by the time I got involved," says Ike. "In a movie, especially in an animated one, all the scenery is fake. But how to make it feel as real as possible is where I come in. We talked about if it came to the darker versus the lighter side of the spectrum, and we would err on the lighter side. Which really plays up the contrast between what Suzu might be experiencing as a character versus her immediate surroundings."

In contrast to Suzu's cluttered bedroom and the quiet Shikoku countryside, Kei and Tomo live in an impersonal structure in Tokyo. "Suzu's house and Kei and Tomo's dwelling are almost polar opposites: For Suzu, there's a suppression and a sense of despair, but beyond that, there's a sense of discovery," explains Hosoda. "For Kei and Tomo, the house serves as a kind of prison. Ike and I talked at length about the houses and what they represent. Depicting Kochi was a big challenge for him, because his work on Satoshi Kon's films focused on Tokyo cityscapes

and loneliness. Kei and Tomo's house is right up Ike's alley: cityscape, despair, loneliness. It checks all the boxes he's good at."

Kochi and Tokyo are far apart, geographically and culturally, but Belle's song bridges the gap. When she discovers Kei's plight, Suzu tries to reach out to him as Belle. But he rejects her, snarling that many people promised to help him, "but nothing changes!"

Shinobu tells her, "Sing to him as yourself. . . . Call out to him as yourself, Suzu." As Belle's concert begins, Justin, who has been trying to destroy the Dragon, appears. He uses a special light as a weapon: It strips away the fantasies of U to reveal people as they really are. Desperate to save Kei and Tomo, Suzu forces him to shine the light on Belle. The glittering diva she worked so hard to create vanishes, leaving an ordinary high school girl in her place.

But when she sings as herself, Suzu touches her audience as never before. She sings to the abused boy she wants to protect—and to the little girl inside herself who is still grieving for her mother. As she sings, Kamishin, with help from Luka, Shinobu, and Hiro, locates Kei's building in Tokyo. Older women who were friends of Suzu's mother call protective services—who say they can't rescue Kei and Tomo immediately. With new determination, Suzu boards the train for Tokyo. Braving a downpour, she finds Tomo and Kei and faces down their brutal father. She proves herself to be her mother's daughter: Someone willing to put herself at risk to save another from peril.

Suzu's victory over the abusive father—and her own inner demons—as herself, rather than as Belle, recalls the words of psychologist Bruno Bettelheim: "Each fairy tale is a magic mirror which reflects some aspects of our inner world, and of the steps required by our evolution from immaturity to maturity. For those who immerse themselves in what the fairy tale has to communicate, it becomes a deep, quiet pool which at first seems to reflect only our own image; but behind it we soon discover the inner turmoils of our soul—its depth, and ways to gain peace within ourselves and with the world, which is the reward of our struggles." Suzu will continue to perform for her audience's pleasure and her own, but she no longer needs to hide behind a character. She has the confidence to be who she is.

Although Hosoda used music with lyrics in his previous features, *Belle* is his first film that could be described as a musical. The songs and performances are woven into the narrative.

"This isn't a movie about singing," he cautions. "The singing links us to the Internet world, where something can change the world. And that something is music. The music director, whom I haven't worked with before, is Taisei Iwasaki—who worked with Ludvig Forsell, Yuta Bandoh, and Miho Hazama. He's thought a lot about how cinema and music relate, and it's been a very good partnership."

For the crucial role of Belle, Hosoda chose not a live-action star, as many American animation directors might, or a professional voice actor, but a musician. "Kaho Nakamura is not an actress or voice actress, but she has a huge range of expression," Hosoda says. "Although she has no acting experience whatsoever, she beat out a lot of industry veterans to land the role through an audition. I'm betting on her range of expression to carry this movie."

Usually, the songs for a film are among the first scenes the artists animate. They're written in advance, as the story is being worked out. "For someone to compose the song, then animate to it would definitely be the way to approach the scene. It really should have been the first thing that we did," Hosoda sighs.

"But for *Belle*, we couldn't do that. The songs weren't completed in advance," he continues. "The composer said, 'I need to see more imagery before I can imagine what the song would sound like.' I wanted to storyboard the movie after I heard the song, so I could get into Belle's world.

BELOW Hosoda's storyboard panel specifies the setting for Suzu's house, but it is an unremarkable dwelling, unlike the architecturally sophisticated house in *Mirai*.

BOTTOM A fully rendered background

Suzu's house stands on a hill in a village deep in the mountains.

It is lit by the morning sun.

But there was no music, so I just had to do the storyboard. Despite all the challenges and chaos, somehow everything fits together in the end in animation, which is a really interesting aspect of what we do."

As Hosoda predicted, things ultimately fit together. The composers completed the song before the animation began. The film progressed on its rather frantic schedule, and in the spring of 2021, Hosoda began editing, working once again with Shigeru Nishiyama.

"I work with Hosoda every three years or so, and there's a span of three or four months that we spend in close proximity to each other," Nishiyama says. "Every time that happens, it's as if my entire body gets molded into a Hosoda setup. After I finish that job and transition to the next one, I have to go through a period of rehab almost . . . just the way I cut sequences, the way things get assembled."

Reflecting on Hosoda's most technically and visually complex film to date, Saito says, "During production on *Wolf Children*, he was concerned that using CG to animate the flowers would give them a different look. He handed the art director and the CG team a single sketch and asked them to add movement to the flowers without altering or weakening the aesthetics of the scene. CG director Ryo Horibe and his team rose to the challenge each time, although it always seemed like an impossible task."

"Two years ago, I talked about how this hand-drawn art form needed to either shift perspective or it was going to be tricky to keep it alive in Japan," Hosoda concludes. "For *Belle*, we wanted to push the boundaries of the artwork, gathering a lot of talented people and pursuing a more fine arts route. We also moved toward a transition to digital expression. I thought it was time to find a new form of expression within the digital space and aesthetic."

Although the COVID pandemic complicated the production, *Belle* was completed on schedule. The film premiered at Cannes, the most prestigious film festival in the world, on July 16—and received a fourteen-minute standing ovation.

The early reviews for *Belle* were universally favorable: For *IndieWire*, David Ehrlich wrote, "At its core, *Belle* is a delirious fusion between a tale as old as time and

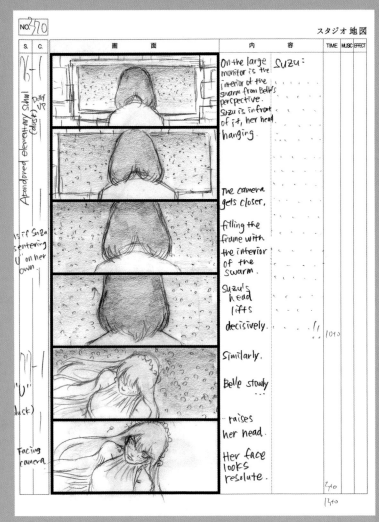

NO. 370

S.C. | 画面 | 内容 | TIME | MUSIC | EFFECT | スタジオ 地図

- On the large monitor is the interior of the swarm from Belle's perspective. Suzu is in front of it, her head hanging. — Suzu:
- The camera gets closer,
- filling the frame with the interior of the swarm.
- Suzu's head lifts decisively.
- Similarly, Belle slowly
- raises her head.
- Her face looks resolute.

(left margin) Abandoned elementary school (dusk) · Is it Suzu entering "U" on her own · "U" (dusk) · Facing camera

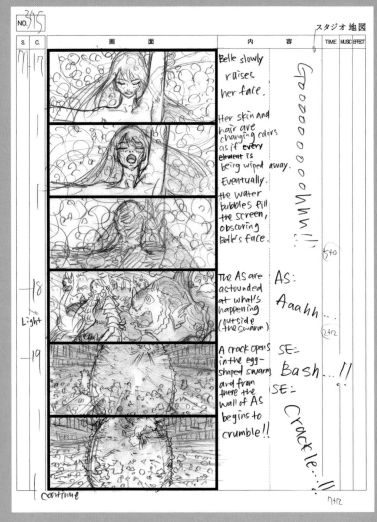

NO. 375

- Belle slowly raises her face.
- Her skin and hair are changing colors as if every element is being wiped away. Eventually, the water bubbles fill the screen, obscuring Belle's face.
- The AS are astounded at what's happening (outside the swarm) — AS: Aaahh...
- A crack opens in the egg-shaped swarm and from there the wall of AS begins to crumble!! — SE: Bash...!! SE: Crackle...!!

Goooooooohhh!!

Continue

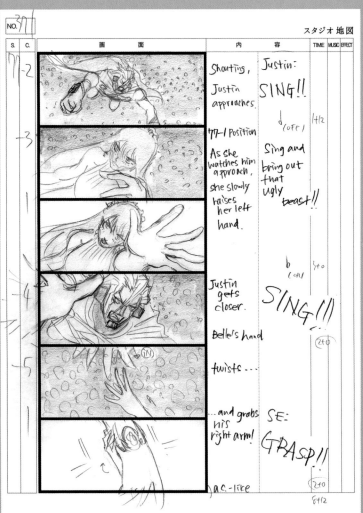

NO. 377

- Shouting, Justin approaches. — Justin: SING!!
- 77-1 Position
- As she watches him approach, she slowly raises her left hand. — Sing and bring out that ugly beast!!
- Justin gets closer. — SING!!
- Belle's hand
- twists...
- ...and grabs his right arm! — SE: GRASP!!

AC-like

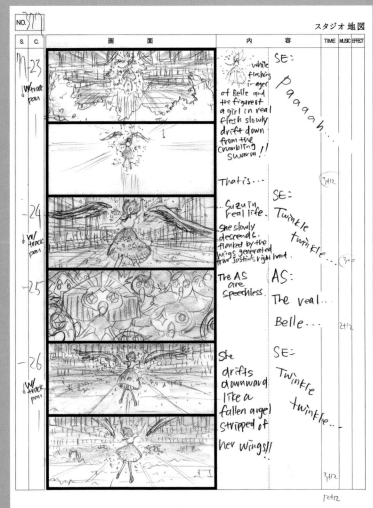

NO. 377

- White flashing images of Belle and the figure of a girl in real flesh slowly drift down from the crumbling swarm!! — SE: Paaah...
- That is...
- Suzu in real life. She slowly descends, flanked by two wings generated from Justin's right hand. — SE: Twinkle twinkle...
- The AS are speechless. — AS: The real... Belle...
- She drifts downward like a fallen angel stripped of her wings!! — SE: Twinkle twinkle...

242

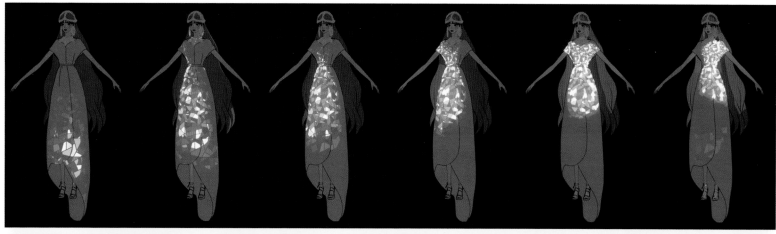

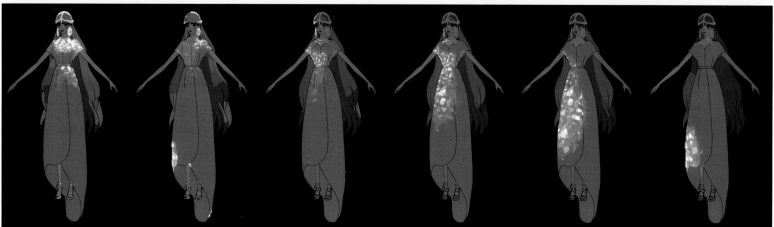

technology that's yet to be invented—one set in a world where everyone is desperate to be visible, but deeply afraid of being seen." Rafael Motamayor of *Collider* wrote, "It would have been very easy for Hosoda to just give *Belle* a Disney aesthetic and call it a day, but instead he gives us his most visually stunning and varied film to date, as well as the best-looking animated movie of the year." Robbie Collin of the *Daily Telegraph* concluded, "There is usually a movie at every Cannes that crushes me emotionally, and this year it was *Belle*. . . . *Belle* is a beautifully observed, dazzlingly animated sci-fi fairy tale about our online-offline double lives—it's Hosoda's finest film since 2012's *Wolf Children*, and perhaps his best to date."

Despite pandemic-related restrictions on audience sizes, *Belle* opened to impressive business in Japan. In the first six days, it was seen by more than 923,000 people in 416 theaters (including 38 IMAX theaters), earning ¥1,312,562,000 (about $12 million), a record for a film of Hosoda's. It quickly became his most successful film to date. Toho Cinemas issued a special souvenir booklet for the opening; Uniqlo released a line of T-shirts with images from Hosoda's films; and Millennium Parade's video "U" topped the Japanese music charts.

Looking back on their working relationship that began with *The Girl Who Leapt Through Time*, Nishiyama reflects, "I feel like Hosoda went from being a challenger to a champion. To say he's carrying the next generation of the anime industry on his shoulders might be an exaggeration, but I think there's an element of truth to it."

OPPOSITE Suzu sacrifices her image as Belle to save Kei, in Hosoda's storyboards.

ABOVE Tests for lighting patterns on one of Belle's gowns

BELOW GKIDS president Eric Beckman, Mamoru Hosoda, and Yuichiro Saito celebrate the premiere of *Belle* at the 2021 Cannes Film Festival.

FOLLOWING SPREAD The modular equator, outsize crescent moon, and twilight skies greet visitors to U.

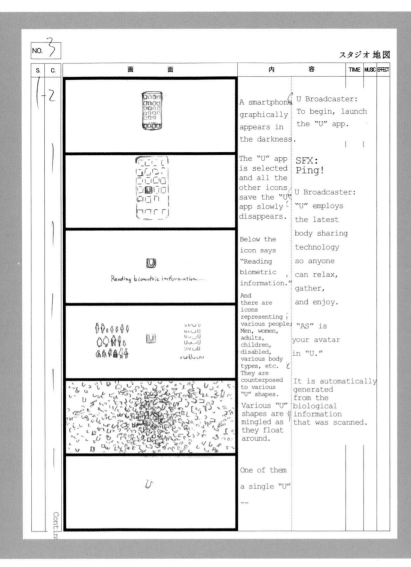

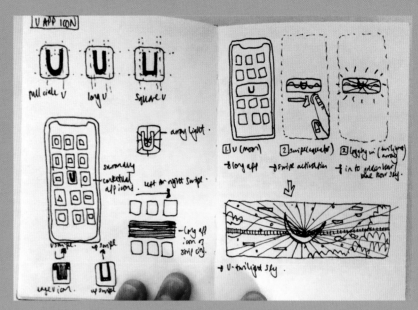

U APP ICON

ABOVE LEFT Hosoda's storyboards use a cell phone as the entry to U.

ABOVE RIGHT Wong begins to explore ideas for the imagery in these pages from his sketchbook.

RIGHT Wong's early experiments with different colors and icons, imagining how users would access U. The initial designs had to be revised when Hosoda sent a note pointing that the icons were arranged in lines of four, not three, on his phone.

OPPOSITE, TOP LEFT Hosoda's storyboard shows Belle entering U.

OPPOSITE, TOP RIGHT Wong's sketches of possible gateway designs

OPPOSITE, BOTTOM Wong initially envisioned a complex gateway built around the shapes of a keyhole and the letter U.

U APP GATEWAY

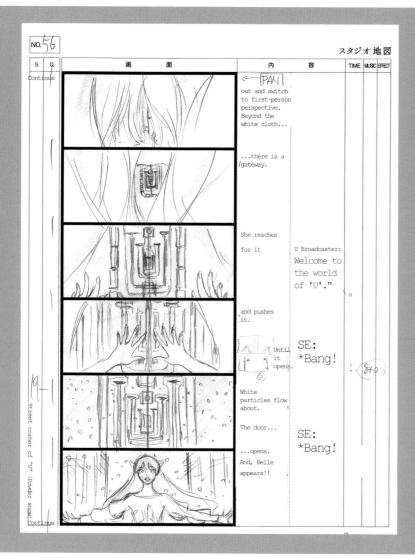

NO.56					
S. q.	画面	内容	TIME	MUSIC	EFFECT

PAN out and switch to first-person perspective. Beyond the white cloth...

...there is a gateway.

She reaches for it

U Broadcaster: Welcome to the world of 'U'.

and pushes it.

Until it opens.

SE: *Bang!

White particles flow about.

The door...

SE: *Bang!

...opens. And, Belle appears!!

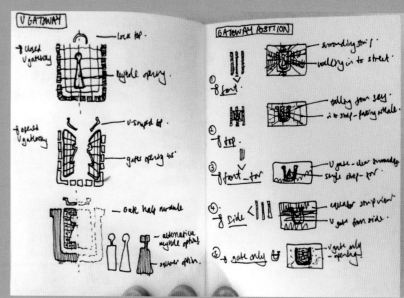

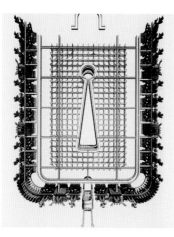

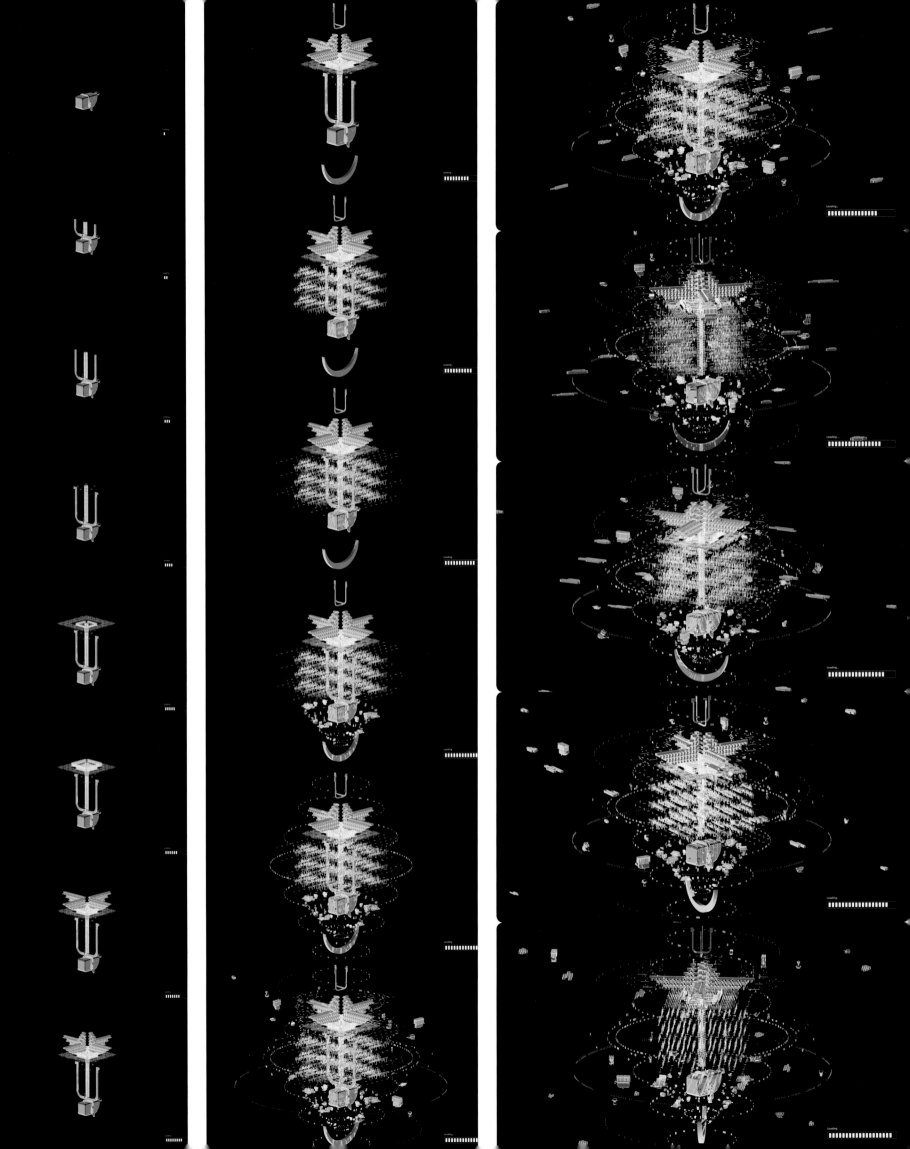

UNIVERSE OF U CONFIGURATIONS

Hosoda initially described U as "having no heaven or earth, no up or down, no left or right."

OPPOSITE Stages in building a structure that fit that description

THIS PAGE Various stages in building that version of U. The artists later decided on a more horizontal image.

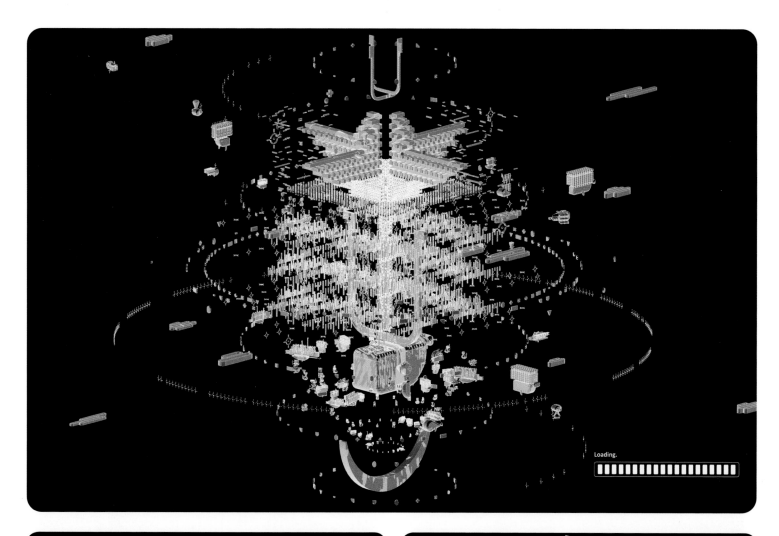

Loading.

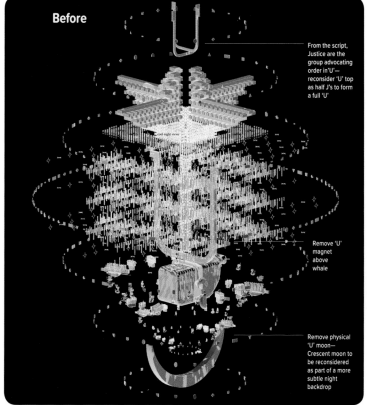

Before

From the script, Justice are the group advocating order in 'U'— reconsider 'U' top as half J's to form a full 'U'

cool night view

Remove 'U' magnet above whale

Remove physical 'U' moon— Crescent moon to be reconsidered as part of a more subtle night backdrop

After

City Strip_Section

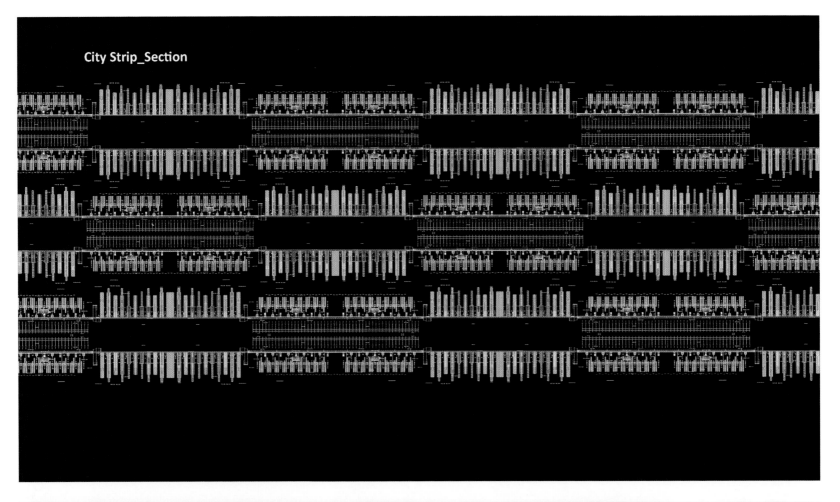

City Strip_Full Module

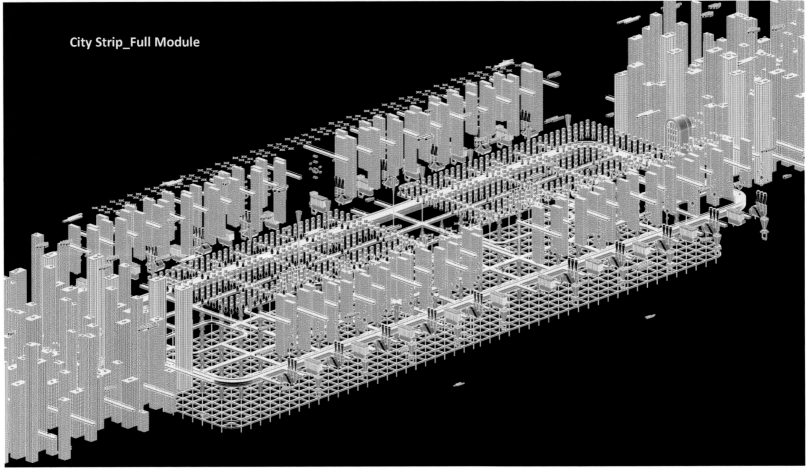

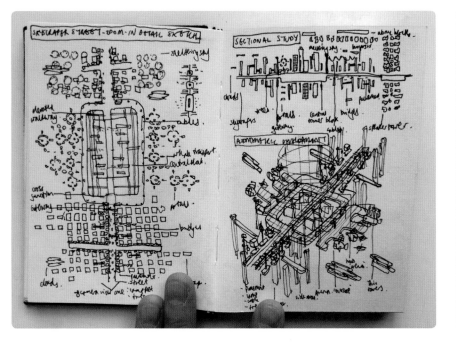

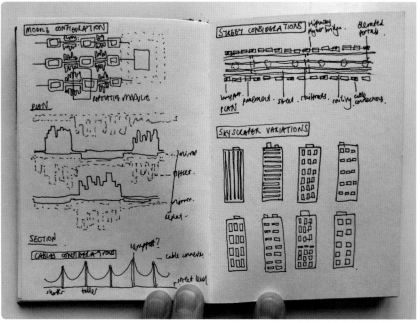

OPPOSITE, TOP Wong explores how the modules that make up the design would stack together.

OPPOSITE, BOTTOM An axiometric projection of one full module

TOP Pages from designer Eric Wong's sketchbook show his early ideas for the look of U.

ABOVE The final background suggests both the infinite possibilities the Internet offers—and its isolation.

THE CASTLE
OF THE DRAGON

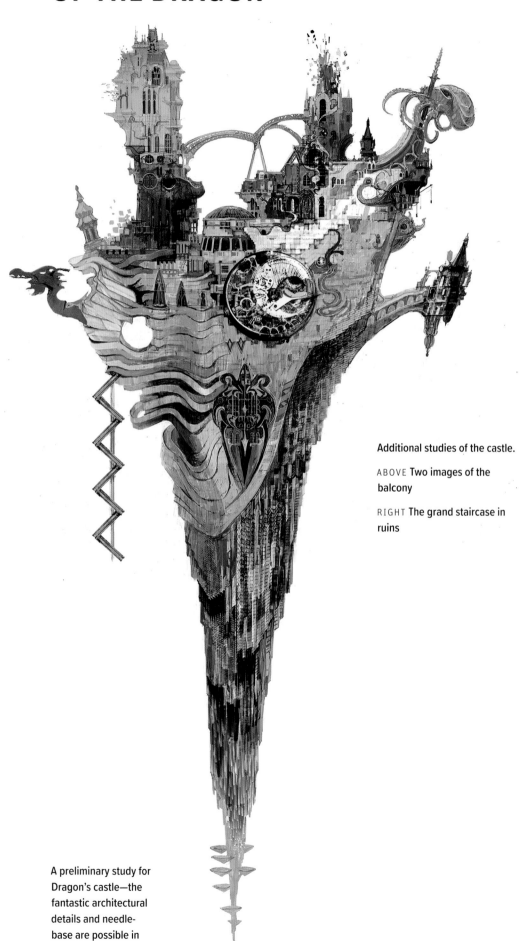

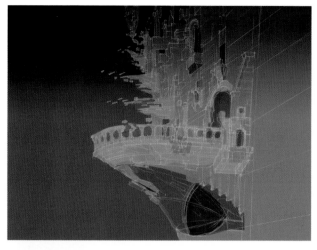

Additional studies of the castle.

ABOVE Two images of the balcony

RIGHT The grand staircase in ruins

A preliminary study for Dragon's castle—the fantastic architectural details and needle-base are possible in the cyber world.

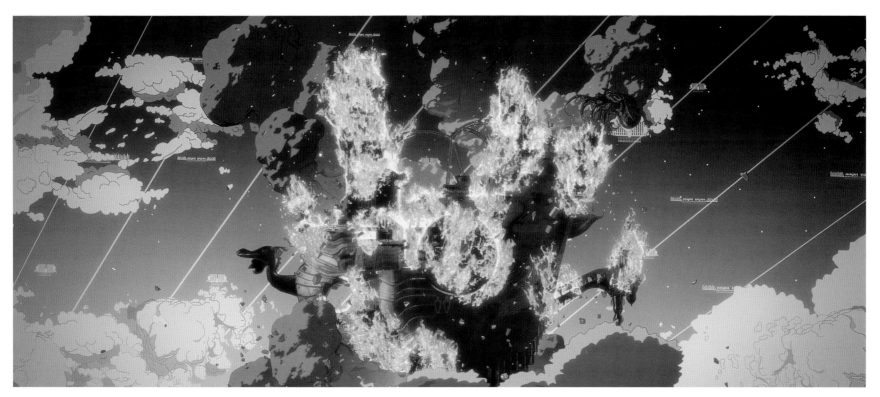

TOP The ballroom of the Dragon's castle, lit to suggest night

ABOVE The Dragon's castle burns after the attack by Justin and his vigilante squad.

CHARACTER DESIGN

Belle in her extravagant cape and gown.
Artist : Jin Kim

OPPOSITE An early study for the Dragon
suggests a collage of patterns.
Artist: Kageichi Akiya

Two early studies of the Dragon show the artist exploring his costume, proportions and posture. Artist: Kageichi Akiya.

OPPOSITE The rich but tattered cloak, hunched shoulders, and hanging head suggest the Dragon's melancholy loneliness. Artist: Kageichi Akiya

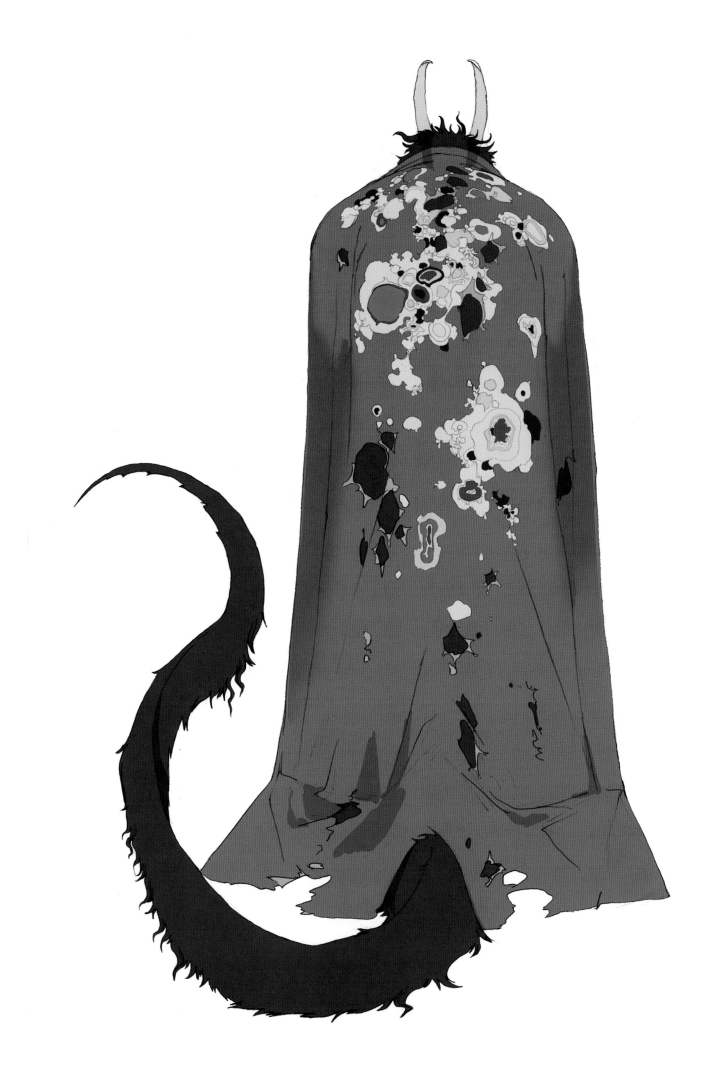

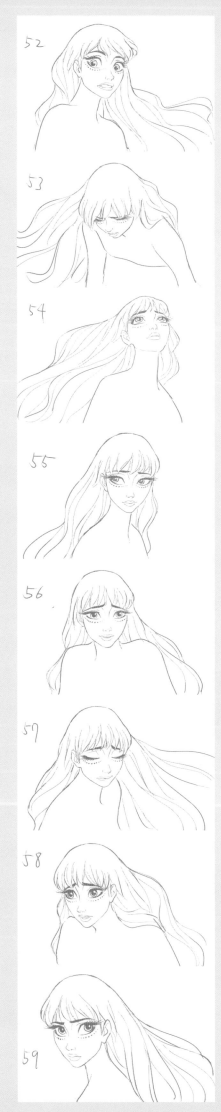

OPPOSITE These sensitive animation drawings by Takaaki Yamashita suggest the magic of Belle's performance.

ABOVE When she visits his hidden castle, Belle tries to discover the source of the Dragon's deep sorrow.

UNIVERSE OF U CHARACTERS

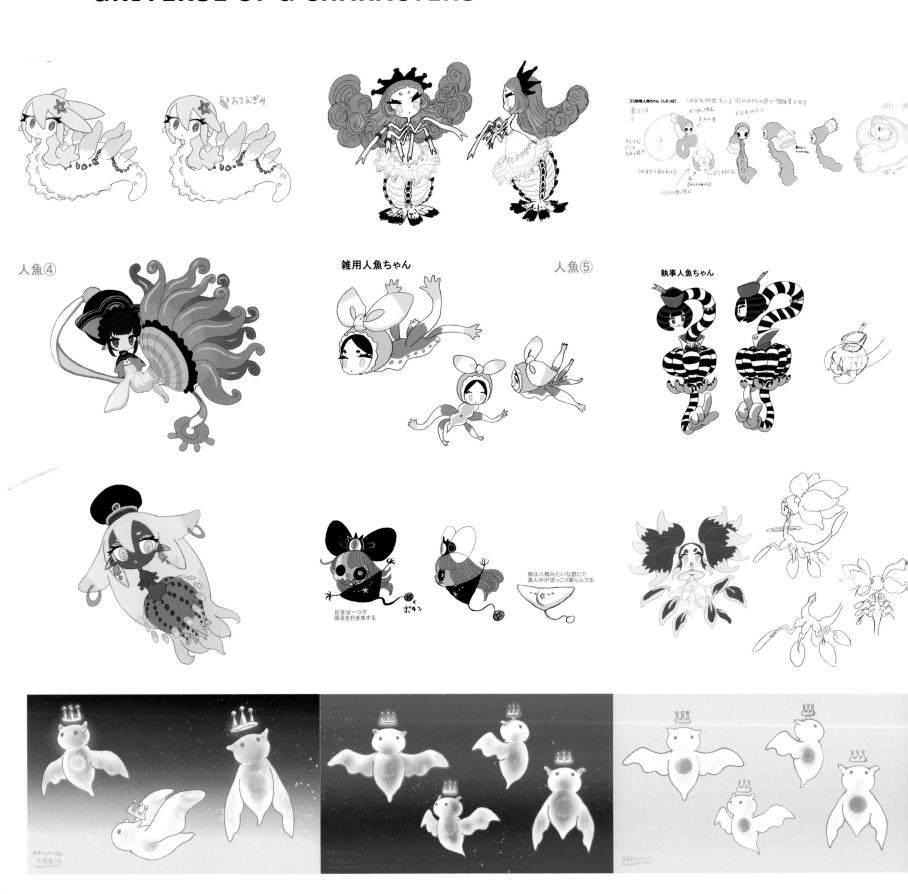

The creatures that inhabit U recall
the avatars in OZ in *Summer Wars*,
but the designs are more complex.

WHALE

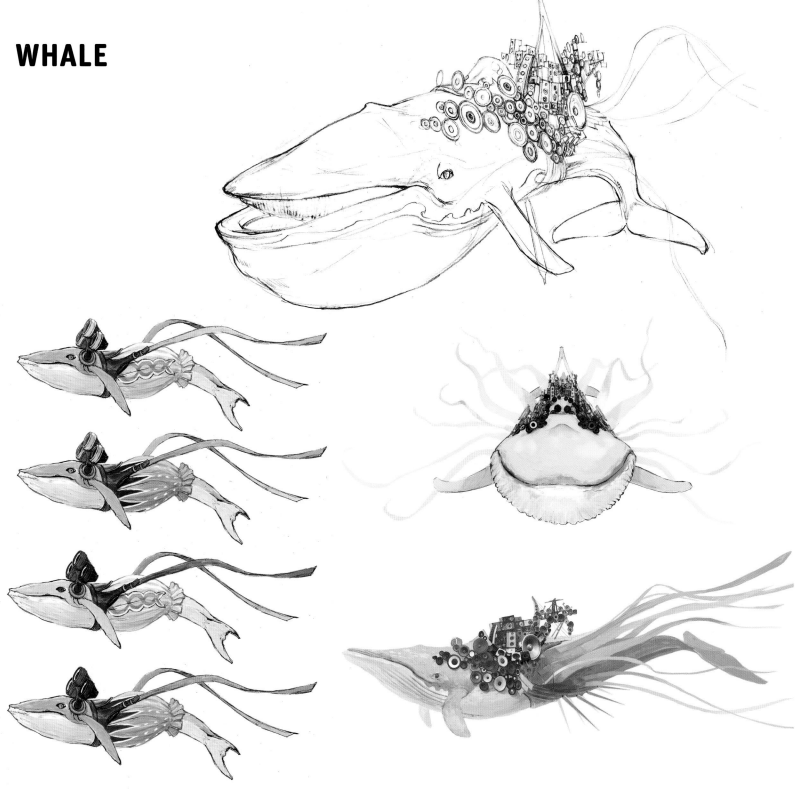

In her showstopping entrance, Belle rides atop a humpback whale equipped with banks of speakers—a spectacle even Lady Gaga can't match.

FOREST & OCEAN

RIGHT Hosoda's storyboards indicate that the Dragon's servants would create mazes to confuse visitors to his castle.

FAR RIGHT AND BELOW Artists at the Irish studio Cartoon Saloon designed the illusory landscapes: The brightly colored pastel layers suggest paper cutouts.

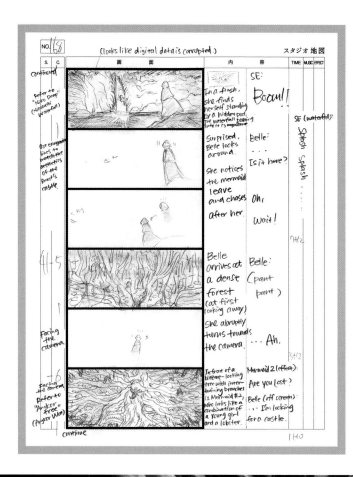

MARKETING

Related merchandise for *Belle* included pens, buttons, T-shirts, and small plush charms of the characters that could be hung on students' backpacks.

OPPOSITE The advance poster for the film suggested the drama of the story—and the complex realm of U.

When asked "What's your favorite of the films you've directed, and which was the most challenging film you directed?" Hosoda summarizes his attitude toward filmmaking when he replies, "It will always be the next one. Previously, *Mirai* was the best and most challenging film. Currently, *Belle* is the best and most challenging film. It'll always be the next work."

ACKNOWLEDGMENTS

This book began over a dinner at Lowery's in Beverly Hills: I complained to producer Yuichiro Saito that there was only one book on Hosoda's work in a Western language (French) and it contained mistakes—including blaming Kenji for cracking the OZ security code in *Summer Wars*. He replied, "You write a better one."

I had already interviewed Mamoru Hosoda several times for various publications, beginning with a story on *Summer Wars* for the *Los Angeles Times*. It was the first of his films I saw, and I was impressed by its graphic brilliance and original storytelling. When Peter Debruge and Eric Beckman asked me to take part in the Animation Is Film Festival in Hollywood, I was able to meet Hosoda-san and Saito-san. We subsequently became friends through question-and-answer sessions, dinners, and visits to other animation artists. My thanks to them both for taking the time for interviews during the creation of *Belle*.

Additional thanks are due at Studio Chizu to Yuya Machida, who scheduled interviews and conferences, and to Laëtitia Gokura, who located the amazing artwork in Chizu archive.

Across the Pacific, Mike McNamara also dealt with scheduling issues (complicated by the International Dateline) and served as interpreter with consummate skill. My patient sensei Ken Endo provided additional help with translations.

My sincere thanks to all the artists and executives affiliated with Studio Chizu who took time from their work for interviews: Hiroyuki Aoyama, Ryo Horibe, Daisuke Iga, Nobutaka Ike, Anri Jojo, Jin Kim, Shigeru Nishiyama, Masakatsu Takagi, Nozomu Takahashi, Yohei Takamatsu, Eric Wong, Takaaki Yamashita. Additional artists who graciously shared their thoughts include Ralph Eggleston, Paul Felix, Glen Keane, Tomm Moore, and David Silverman. Special thanks to my friend Don Hahn for his foreword.

My excellent agent Richard Curtis oversaw the contract. Greg Pincus transcribed the interviews with his accustomed speed and precision. Eric Klopfer at Abrams once again proved to be a singularly patient and sympathetic editor. Designer Shawn Dahl thoughtfully and beautifully brought the book to life.

I remain grateful for my friends' continuing forbearance when I fuss about writing: Julian Bermudez, Kevin Caffey, Pete Docter, Paul Felix, Eric and Susan Goldberg, Dennis Johnson, Jef Mallett, John Rabe, Stuart Sumida. On the home front, special thanks are due Scott and Matter; additional editing was provided by Typo, who insists my keyboard is a secondary cat bed.

Charles Solomon

BIBLIOGRAPHY

Books

Bloton, Christopher. *Interpreting Anime*. Minneapolis: University of Minnesota Press, 2018.

Chiu, Pa Ming. *Mamoru Hosoda*. Réalité Augmentée. Paris: Ynnis Éditions, 2018.

Hosoda, Mamoru. *The Boy & The Beast*. Translated by Sawa Matsueda. New York: YenOn, 2016.

———. *Mirai*. Translated by Winifred Bird. New York: YenOn, 2018.

———. *Summer Wars Material Book*. Translated by M. Kirie Hayashi. Richmond Hill, ON: Udon Entertainment, 2009.

———. *Wolf Children Ame & Yuki*. Translated by Winifred Bird. New York: YenOn, 2012.

Mizuki, Shigeru. *The Birth of Kitaro*. Translated by Zack Davisson. New York: Drawn & Quarterly, 2016.

Tsutsui, Yasutaka. *The Girl Who Leapt Through Time*. Translated by David Karashima. Richmond, UK: Alma Books, 2011.

Articles

A.B. "L'arbre Ghibli et la forêt japonaise." *Le Figaro Magazine*, June 5, 2010.

Abrams, Simon. "The Boy and the Beast." RogerEbert.com, March 4, 2016.

Blair, Gavin J. "Anime Director Mamoru Hosoda on Drawing by Hand and the Industry Post–Hayao Miyazaki." *Hollywood Reporter*, November 11, 2016.

Burr, Ty. "Time Stands Still in Enchanting 'Girl.'" *Boston Globe*, August 22, 2008.

Cena, Mathias. "Le réalisateur Mamoru Hosoda: 'Je ne pouvais pas être éternel-lement un fan de Miyzaki.'" *20 Minutes*, December 17, 2017.

Chapuis, Marius, and Mamoru Hosoda. "Il est impossible de porter un sensibilité divergente au sein du studio Ghibli." *Liberation*, December 25, 2018.

Collin, Robbie. "First-Rate Animation Finds Hidden Magic in the Gaps of Everyday Life." *Daily Telegraph*, November 1, 2018.

Coomes, Nina Li. "The Oscar-Nominated *Mirai* Is More Than a Moving Tale of Childhood." *Atlantic*, February 18, 2019.

Creamer, Nick. "The Girl Who Leapt Through Time." Anime News Network, June 27, 2016.

Debruge, Peter. "Anime Master Mamoru Hosoda Invents an Enchanted Way for an Only Child to Come Around to the Idea of Sharing His Home with a Baby Sister." *Variety*, June 15, 2018.

———. "The Boy and the Beast." *Variety*, September 23, 2015.

———. "Mirai." *Variety*, June 14, 2018.

Delorme, Gérard. "Summer Wars de Mamoru Hosoda." *Première*, June 2010.

Douhaire, Samuel. "Panique chez les geeks." *Télérama*, June 9, 2010.

Dudok de Wit, Alex. "Mamoru Hosoida Teams Up with Cartoon Saloon and Disney Vet Jin Kim for New Film 'Belle.'" *Cartoon Brew*, April 2, 2021.

Ebiri, Bilge. "A Charming Animated Trip into a Family's Past." *New York Times*, November 29, 2018.

Ellwood, Gregory. "The Animated 'Mirai' Takes the Life of a Real Boy and Laces It with the Fantastical." *Los Angeles Times*, January 29, 2019.

Felperin, Leslie. " 'Mirai' ('Mirai, My Little Sister')." *Hollywood Reporter*, May 25, 2018.

Fallaix, Olivier. "Mamrou Hosoda: Summer Wars." AnimeLand, June 2010.

Hall, Sandra. "*Boy and the Beast* Review: Realism Enters the Fantastic Hand of Mamoru Hosoda." *Sydney Morning Herald*, March 1, 2016.

Henderson, Tim. "Summer Wars: Blu-Ray." Anime News Network, May 18, 2011.

Hikawa, Ryusuke. "Interview with Mamoru Hosoda." *Freestyle Magazine*, June 30, 2007. (氷川 隆介。インタビューアー。フリースタイル マガジン。発 売日2007年6月30日) translated by Ken Endo.

Ide, Wendy. " 'Mirai' Cannes Review: Charming Animation from Japan Takes a Toddler-Eye View of a New Arrival in the Family." Screendaily, May 16, 2018.

Keslassy, Elsa. "Gaumont Dives into Japanese Animation with Mamoru Hosoda's 'The Boy and the Beast.'" *Variety*, December 12, 2014.

———. "Mamoru Hosoda's 'Belle' Lures Top-Notch International Creative Team and Unveils First Trailer." *Variety*, April 1, 2021.

Koffel, Laurent. "Interview: Mamoru Hosoda." *Coyote Magazine*, July 27, 2016.

Lorrain, François-Guillaume. "Cinema: Artillerie lourde." *Le Point*, June 10, 2010.

Mingot, Jérémy. "Mamoru Hosoda (Miraï, ma petite soeur): 'Ce film m'a été inspiré par mes propres enfants!'" *Télé-Loisirs*, December 25, 2018.

Odicino, Guillemette. " ' Miraï, ma petite soeur': Mamoru Hosoda signe un merveilleux film sur la famille." *Télérama*, December 26, 2018.

Robey, Tim. "The Japanese Anime Film 'Wolf Children' Is a Hauntingly Romantic Fairytale." *Daily Telegraph*, October 24, 2013.

Roe, Matthew. "Ranking the Films of Mamoru Hosoda." Anime News Network, November 30, 2018.

Saito, Stephen. "Interview: Mamoru Hosoda on Tapping into His Inner Child for 'Mirai.'" *The Moveable Feast*, November 30, 2018.

Saltz, Rachel. "Young Math Wizard Stumbles Upon OZ, Deep in the Heart of the Internet." *New York Times*, December 28, 2010.

"Samouraïs virtuels." *Le Monde Magazine*, June 12, 2010.

"Summer Wars l'été RPG." AnimeLand, June, 2010.

Schilling, Mark. "Could 'Shoplifters' or 'Mirai' Pick Up an Oscar? The Chances Are Slim but Real." *Japan Times*, February 14, 2019.

———. "The Future King of Japanese Animation May Be with Us: Hosoda Steps Out of Miyazaki's Shadow with Dazzling New Film." *Japan Times*, August 7, 2009.

———. "Okami Kodomo no Ame to Yuki (Wolf Children)." *Japan Times*, July 20, 2012.

———. "Tokyo International Film Festival Welcomes Audiences to the Animated World of Mamoru Hosoda." *Japan Times*, October 26, 2016.

Schley, Matt. " 'Mirai:' Mamoru Hosoda's latest anime is for the young at heart." *Japan Times*, June 25, 2018.

Sevakis, Justin. "The Girl Who Leapt Through Time." Anime News Network, March 5, 2007.

———. "Summer Wars." Anime News Network, November 27, 2009.

Solomon, Charles. "Animated 'Boy and the Beast' Draws on Emotional Depth to Rise Above Typical Martial Arts Saga." *Los Angeles Times*, December 3, 2015.

———. "Anime Review: Mamoru Hosoda Movie Collection." *Animation Scoop*, November 6, 2018.

———. "Mamoru Hosoda Q & A @ Animation Is Film Festival." Funimation, October 30, 2018.

———. " 'Mirai': Adventures in Time Travel with Mamoru Hosoda." *Animation Magazine*, December, 2018.

Sotinel, Thomas. " 'Miraï, ma petite soeur' psyché enfantine à grand spectacle." *Le Monde*, December 26, 2018.

Thomas, Kevin. "Summer Wars." *Los Angeles Times*, January 6, 2011.

Travers, Peter. "Animated Boy-and-Baby Sister Tale Hits Heartstring Bull's Eye." *Rolling Stone*, November 28, 2018.

Turan, Kenneth. "Mamoru Hosoda's 'Wolf Children' Anime Is Wild." *Los Angeles Times*, September 26, 2013.

———. "The Playfully Imaginative Anime 'Mirai' Tells a Family Story That's Not Just for Kids." *Los Angeles Times*, November 29, 2018.

Vié, Caroline. "'Le garçon et al bête'": Et si Mamoru Hosoda devenait le nouveau Miyazaki?" *20 Minutes*, January 13, 2016.

Yoshida, Emily. "'Mirai' Is a Galaxy-Brained Journey Through a Family's Past and Future." Vulture, November 30, 2018.

Yu, Michelle. "The Girl Who Leapt Through Time." Anime News Network, February 20, 2011.

ABOUT THE AUTHOR

An internationally respected critic and historian of animation, **Charles Solomon** has written for the *New York Times*, *Newsweek* (Japan), the *Los Angeles Times*, *Variety*, and National Public Radio. His books include *The Art of Wolf-Walkers* (2020), *Tale as Old as Time: The Art and Making of Disney's Animated Classic Beauty and the Beast* (2017), *The Art of the Disney Golden Books* (2014), *The Art and Making of Peanuts Animation: Celebrating Fifty Years of Television Specials* (2012), *The Toy Story Films: An Animated Journey* (2012), *The Disney That Never Was* (1995), and *Enchanted Drawings: The History of Animation* (1989), which was a *New York Times* Notable Book of the Year and the first book to be nominated for a National Book Critics Circle Award. Solomon also teaches the history of animation at UCLA and Chapman University.

Disney production designer Paul Felix's caricature of the author as an avatar from OZ in *Summer Wars*

EDITOR **Eric Klopfer**

DESIGNER **Shawn Dahl, dahlimama inc**

MANAGING EDITOR **Annalea Manalili**

PRODUCTION MANAGER **Denise LaCongo**

Library of Congress Control Number: 2021932560

ISBN: 978-1-4197-5372-5
eISBN: 978-1-64700-258-9

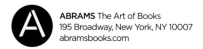

ABRAMS The Art of Books
195 Broadway, New York, NY 10007
abramsbooks.com